The Silent Cry

A Journey from Molestation to Divine Manifestation of Healing

Tracey T. Lancaster

The Silent Cry
© 2024 Tracey Lancaster

All rights reserved. This book or parts thereof may not be reproduced in any form, stored in any retrieval system, or transmitted in any form by any means—electronic, mechanical, photocopy, recording, or otherwise—without prior written permission of the author, except for the use of brief quotations in a book review and as provided by United States of America's copyright law. For permission requests, please refer all questions to the author, Tracey Lancaster, PO Box 1724, White Plains, Maryland 20695: thesilentcryjourney@gmail.com

Contact Tracey Lancaster for information about special discounts available for bulk purchases, sales promotions, fundraising, and educational needs.

The information presented in this book is presented for educational purposes only.

Scripture quotations from The Authorized (King James) Version. Rights in the Authorized Version in the United Kingdom are vested in the Crown. Reproduced by permission of the Crown's patentee, Cambridge University Press

The Voice Bible Copyright © 2012 Thomas Nelson, Inc. The Voice™ translation © 2012 Ecclesia Bible Society. All rights reserved.

The Passion Translation®. Copyright © 2017, 2018, 2020 by Passion & Fire Ministries, Inc. Used by permission. All rights reserved. ThePassionTranslation.com.

All Scripture quotations, unless otherwise indicated, are taken from the Amplified Bible (AMPCE), Copyright © 1954, 1958, 1962, 1964, 1965, 1987 by The Lockman Foundation. Used by permission.

Scripture quotations are from The ESV® Bible (The Holy Bible, English Standard Version®), © 2001 by Crossway, a publishing ministry of Good News Publishers. Used by permission. All rights reserved.

Scripture taken from the Good News Translation in Today's English Version-Second Edition Copyright © 1992 by American Bible Society. Used by Permission.

Cover design by Joshua Peter

Printed in the United States of America
ISBN: 978-1-955253-17-8

Advance Praise

After reading, I thanked God for my wife's strength and courage to write this book.

If you are a husband, father, brother, uncle, or friend, this book will open your eyes to things your female relatives may have faced. It's not even limited to gender. Many men hide the fact that they have been abused out of fear, pride, or something else. Don't miss the opportunity to shame the devil. This book will open your spirit and mind to the enemy's devices.

As Tracey's husband, I couldn't help but feel a sense of insurmountable rage at what she had gone through, seeing her struggle from her eyes. The devil and I were genuinely warring with each other during my read. However, as I continued to read, the love of God replaced my anger, and I realized what it took for my wife to come to trust God as her deliverer, healer, and comforter. I have come to understand my wife more. I have come to understand God more. At the end of this book, I genuinely hope that you will come to understand God in a deeper and more meaningful way.

James T. Lancaster, Husband

Reading the book allowed me to hear about my mother's experiences as a young child. Reading these things truly angered me, asking, "Where were the adults?" "You mean to tell me nobody knew?" As a mother now, I couldn't imagine any of my children experiencing this silent cry. The pain, the abuse, the torment mentally, physically, and emotionally.

As a believer in Christ, I've learned that open doors lead to planted seeds that will affect our generational bloodline. If these generational curses aren't destroyed, they will continue to manifest and create brokenness—a life of oppression instead of walking in our birthright of abundance. When we receive Jesus Christ as our Lord and Savior, He blesses us with many promises written in His Word.

I say to any man, woman, or child who has experienced this kind of abuse, it's not the end! Mend your broken pieces together by developing a relationship with God, and if you seek someone to talk to, ensure you receive godly counseling. Allow your pain to birth your purpose. I pray that those who read this book will find freedom, a voice, and boldness! If my mom can do it, so can you.

I pray reading this book will give you hope, free you from the bondage and shackles, and everything the devil meant for bad will turn around for your good. Let the power of the Blood of Jesus Christ cleanse your generational bloodline so that you and your generation can walk in freedom and the overflow of God's blessings.

Stephanie Davis, Daughter/Realtor

The term story comes from the Latin word historical and is connected to the Old English story, which initially meant a tier of painted windows. When I think of painted windows, I think of the elaborate painted or stained glass in older churches that depict parts of the Bible. As a child, I always admired these "painted windows" because they told a story in a single image. This book is my mother-in-law's "painted window." This book describes the making of Tracey. Allowing others to hear her personal story, no matter how gruesome it may be, is a courageous act. In many cultures, we so often sweep trauma under the rug. We know things are wrong, and we know mental health is real, yet we don't speak about it or do anything about it.

This book speaks volumes to people from all walks of life who have had trauma. It is living proof that you can overcome if you trust in God. You can break the chains that are built to hurt you. It says that God can guide you through your storm and bring you out stronger, healthier, and a better version of yourself than ever if you have faith enough to trust him. It's a book that has given me a tremendous amount of understanding, appreciation, and gratitude to have this woman of God as my mother-in-law. Tracey, I am proud of you and appreciate the opportunity to understand you better!

TiQuanna Patton, Daughter-in-Law

Truthfully, reading this book wasn't easy, but it was necessary. It told the truth about what people go through and how God still works miracles. As pastors, we hear all manner of histories of people, and none quite encapsulates a steady stream of events like this one. We encourage anyone to read this book.

This book shows how things start in people's lives and how they can be free. This is not just a story of molestation but of open doors and strongholds. We thank God that Tracey could come forward with this spiritual knowledge and how God has delivered her from the enemy's plans.

Drs. Kayode and Ola Peter, Abiding Word Global Ministry

This book is not for the faint of heart. It is an honest, riveting, heart-wrenching account of one woman's journey of survival, healing, and faith. She did not let her past define her, and she did not let her abusers win. She fought for her life, her dignity, and her freedom.

This book is a story of tragedy, triumph, courage, resilience, redemption, hope, joy, and peace, and how God can transform a broken life into a beautiful masterpiece. It is an invitation to join the author on her journey of healing and growth.

Minister Krishonda Torres, M.Ed., Abiding Word Global Ministry

When asked to compose a blurb for Tracey Lancaster's book titled, "The Silent Cry," I, too, sought to cry. This book is about the redemption of heart, mind, body, soul, and spirit from the author's life view and, most assuredly, the readers. To certainly know and understand that for a wound to be healed, the Blood of the Lamb of Christ must touch it. You will genuinely discover this as you read "The Silent Cry."

Minister Michelle Christinea, Educator

This book is a remarkable and profound testament to God's unwavering affection for humanity, portraying how staying spiritually aligned with Him can result in deliverance, support, and ultimate salvation from our adversaries. By reading Tracey's inspiring narrative, I was genuinely touched and compelled to examine my journey introspectively, identifying areas where transformations and closures are essential. Tracey emerges as an exemplary and esteemed servant of God, possessing an unwavering commitment to God's will and a remarkable ability to discern His voice. Consequently, anyone who embarks upon this book's profound wisdom and fervent prayers will undoubtedly reap its invaluable guidance and enrichment.

Tomiko Butler, Coordination Officer

I believe this book has come at the right time; while the events are all too familiar for many, the author's transparency is the key to unlocking the silent cry for others. Because the author did not hold back, others will not hold back. Fear and pain have been granted the key to unlock the doors that have been shut too long. Many will receive healing and freedom because one person told all…. now others no longer need to suffer in silence; they can go free.

Jennifer Gregory, Realtor

After experiencing the raw emotions evoked by 'The Silent Cry,' I felt an overwhelming gratitude towards Tracey for her bravery in sharing her story. As I delved into its pages, I realized the universal relevance of its message, transcending gender and shedding light on hidden struggles. Tracey's courageously revealing her spiritual battles and triumphs is a beacon of hope for all seeking liberation from their struggles. This book is not just a narrative of survival; it's a testament to the transformative grace of God, inviting readers to confront their pain, embrace healing, and embark on a path toward freedom and redemption.

Dr. Tony Warrick, Author and Community Advocate

Dedication

I want to dedicate this book to my Real Father, Heavenly Father, Lord and Savior Jesus Christ, and the Precious Holy Spirit. With a grateful heart, thank you for giving me my assignment before I was in my mother's womb, creating me in your image, and instructing and teaching me the way to go. You are guiding me with your eye.

Thank you for not giving up on me when I lived for the world. You gave me the ultimate gift of Salvation so I may have eternal life with you, even when I was unfaithful; you have always been faithful.

Thank you for delivering and healing the wounds of my past and teaching me the importance of forgiving and loving so you, as my Heavenly Father, can forgive me. Thank you for calling me to write this book. I had an ear to hear your voice and followed your instructions obediently. I can't say it enough: thank you for uprooting everything out of my life that was from my past of being molested, which opened doors in my life that only you could teach me how to close and help others to do the same. Thank you.

Thank you for choosing me and teaching me, and most of all, thank you for loving me so much that you gave your only begotten Son, my Lord and Savior Jesus Christ. He gave His Life for me so I may have Life and Life more abundantly.

Thank you so much for the Precious Holy Spirit and the Blood of Jesus Christ.

I thank you for giving me beauty for ashes, the oil of joy for mourning, the garment of praise for the spirit of heaviness. Thank You for being a Loving Heavenly Father

"How God anointed Jesus of Nazareth with the Holy Ghost and with power: who went about doing good, and healing all that were oppressed of the devil; for God was with him." Acts 10:38

Acknowledgments

To my loving husband, I thank God for you and how He blesses our marriage. I appreciate your patience, understanding heart, and being my best friend and partner. This book has revealed things I experienced. Thank you for not judging me during this process of my deliverance and healing. You have experienced how God has delivered and healed me from the wounds of my past bondage, hurt, rejection, abuse, and pain. Thank you for taking the time to hear my story.

To all our children and grand buddies, I thank God for each of you. You have seen and experienced some things in my life, and I want to say I love you all from the bottom of my heart. Your love and support have helped shape me into a better person. I want to say a special thank you to my granddaughter Lauren, aka Glamour-girl. I genuinely appreciate your blessing and helping me proofread my book. To my daughters-in-law, I am so glad you are a part of the family. May God's favor be upon the youngest to the oldest. Always know that Jesus Christ is always with you.

I want to thank all my family, friends, co-workers, spiritual mentors, God's Generals, who have invested in my life, those on the prayer line, and everyone else who has been a blessing to me in many ways.

Thank you, Radeam Conway, Dona Wiggins, Kim, and Sloan Davis, Brenda Grinkley, Dr. Lisa Hugh, Brian and Denise Curry, Robert and Tania Johnson, Theresa McClaude, Allegro Kelsey, and many of you whose name is not listed that have taken time out of your busy schedule to be a blessing to me as I wrote this book. Thank you all so very much.

Drs. Kayode and Ola Peter from Abiding Word Global Ministry, there are not enough words to express my gratitude and appreciation for having you as a part of my spiritual growth. God continues to use you to counsel and nurture me in His Word. While writing this book, I had to go through deliverance and healing, and I want to say a special thank you.

Drs. Chastine and Ella Rock and Pastor Milton from Faith Christian Center World Outreach, thank you for having a special part in my spiritual growth and being a blessing to me.

I love you all and plead the Precious Blood of Jesus Christ over your lives. May God teach each of us and bring His peace to our lives. I pray that each of us will have a supernatural divine encounter with the true and living God. I claim each of your souls for Jesus Christ and that you all have a Supernatural Divine Encounter with the True and Living God. So be it! Amen.

Table of Contents

The Silent Cry 13
The Maze Begins 23
First Love and Broken Curses 33
Strong Family Bonds 43
The Second Chosen One 53
Salvation 65
What Came After 79
Overcoming 88
How to Close Open Doors: Prayer Points 95
- Molestation 99
- Playing House 112
- Abortion 117
- Sexual Immorality to Sexual Transmitted Diseases .. 123
- Everyone Behind the Pulpit Is Not Called By God. ... 127
- Unforgiveness 135
- Be Obedient to the Voice of the Holy Spirit 144

Final Information: Additional Readings 148
About the Author 155

Chapter 1

The Silent Cry

Open doors – it is simply tugging and turning a handle to enter a new room. Doors have been around for centuries, coming in all shapes and forms. But what if I told you there is a different kind of door? One that has been around for much longer. Spiritual open doors are much the same. They have opened entrances that allow things to pass through them. However, spiritual open doors are not so easily shut. They can be opened for years without decaying or closing. It takes a special power to close them and keep them closed.

Many doors can be opened and closed all at once. There are people whose lives are a forest of doors letting in the meekest of sheep to the most violent wolves. For generations, that forest only grows, encompassing not only them but their families as well. The daunting task of closing doors can only be realized with the knowledge of what they are. For some, that knowledge came too late, and for others, it came just in time.

My life was one such forest of open and closed doors; it was more of a maze. Throughout my story, you will see how this life goes from a silent cry to a true blessing.

My grandparents' home was far too crowded growing up. If their home were a state, the cities would consist of my aunt, uncles, mother, brothers, cousins, and myself.

Grandma was famous for being busy on the weekends because sometimes she had to work some Saturdays and Sundays, but when she did manage some spare time, the entire family was blessed with the greatest breakfast of their lives. To this day, I remember the menu: grits, fried potatoes, sausages, bacon, scrapple, scrambled or sunny-side-up eggs with homemade hot biscuits right out of the oven, butter, jelly, and honey. I couldn't forget the gallon of orange drink that washed it all down. Her free weekends didn't consist of breakfast; instead, they consisted of spiritual food—the church. My great-grandmother attended this church many years ago.

Like most kids, I didn't understand the importance of church; I just followed where all the older folks went. Seeing everyone screaming at the top of their lungs, lifting their hands, jumping, and singing looked foreign to me. "What are they feeling?" I wondered. I was too young to understand.

Our extremely close family stood together daily, my grandparents being the glue that united us. Indeed, nothing could separate what we had. It could have simply been our proximity, but family was family.

Then someone invaded our home. It was a family friend who resided at my grandparents' house for quite some time. We'll call him Malcolm. Though the house was crowded, my grandparents did not turn him away. It was so long ago, and I'm not sure of my exact age, but I believe I was around the age of five when he came into our home.

The man slept on a rollaway bed downstairs. Our house started to look more and more like a hotel every day. When the people I loved and respected were gone for part of the day, Malcolm was the designated man in charge.

Nothing stood out about him at first. He was like every other man I knew. He watched the television, primarily sports, and was probably into cars and other things boys would like. He was also, apparently, a responsible person my grandparents trusted.

One day, when the adults were out of the house, I decided to go to my room, which I shared with other family members, to let the boys (my brothers, uncles, cousins, and Malcolm) watch the TV downstairs. I don't quite remember what I was doing, but I remember the distinct sound of the door opening and closing and something like a haze creeping in. When I turned around, I saw Malcolm standing by the door.

Something felt different about him this time. That unassuming feeling I had previously completely shifted into something darker, even disturbing. The feelings soon became justified. He grabbed me and stood me on the dresser, and in seconds, he forced my clothes off, putting his hands anywhere he could feel.

Once the shock wore off, I came to my senses and tried to yell. He whispered, "If you say anything to your family, you won't see them again."

The heat in my body became nothing but ice. What was he going to do to them? Was he going to kill them if I said something? Would he kill me?

I had to force myself into a whisper by letting the tears stream from my eyes as I cried silently for help.

I wished that his attacks would have stopped at touching, but unfortunately, they grew more intense. He would try to force himself inside me, then quickly stop so no one would catch him.

Sadly, it was not that one time; it just continued to repeat itself, and I felt like a puppet. Anytime he appeared in any room when I was alone, the strings would rise, and I dangled helplessly. Each time he repeated his actions, he also repeated his promise: "Say anything, and you'll never see your family again."

His threats took root inside my brain, and every day, I worried for my life. So, I surrendered that my only option was to put up with it.

Here is where a door of hopelessness and anger began to creak open. Did anyone see my suffering? Did they not care? Their little city was up in flames, and yet everyone's lives carried on as if they didn't smell the smoke.

I started isolating myself little by little, and anger built up inside of me since no one noticed my pain. The more it happened, the more anger began to take its roots – and this door led to something else that became wider and more dangerous. Unfortunately, this abuse begins with another family friend.

This family friend lived on the top section of a two-story building with a convenience store below.

One day, this lady came to our house and singled me out to go to the store with her. The strange part about this is that some of my family was there. She could have gone with any of us or multiple people, but she chose me and me alone. We walked to the store, and I thought nothing of it. Instead of going to the convenience store, she took me to her apartment above the store.

The second the door was closed, she started kissing me. She took my clothes off and began to put her hands on my private parts. I wanted to scream. Surely, someone in the store would hear if there was anyone below. But then, she said, "If you say anything to your family, you're not going to see them again." I paused. That same threat again. My young brain was not capable of dealing with being violated once again. I didn't know what to say or what to do.

The only thing I could do was try to keep my tears from escaping me. Who could I tell? Who would care? More fuel was thrown on the burning city, yet no one noticed. After that incident, I became even more sheltered and isolated. No one could see what was happening to me, smell the smoke, or help me put out the fires.

At a time when fire was the only thing I saw, the only sight of water was when my mother finally found a new place for us to move.

It took quite a bit of preparation, but we could finally move. My mother had to apply for low-income housing, and when she was approved, we were well on our way. The house was in the "Projects," located in Southeast DC., a notoriously hard neighborhood that was filled with shootings, drugs, theft, and all manners of negative influences.

My mother didn't know about the area; she just wanted to leave my grandparents' house, which I referred to as a crowded state with many cities of people.

Mixed feelings swelled within me. While I was glad to be away from my abusers, I couldn't help but miss my grandparents so much. Leaving them in the same house as Malcolm and close to that other lady felt wrong, but what else could I do?

Malcolm's presence, in particular, further rubbed salt in the wound as he was among those who helped us move. At that moment, I realized that the greater my distance from him, the better off I was. He was a disgusting human being, I thought. My only prayer was that my grandparents would figure out who he is and send him where he belongs.

When we moved into our new house, I saw an opportunity for a new life. The house had three bedrooms. Being the only girl, I got my own room while my brothers had to share. Most importantly, I could think about how I didn't need to be afraid anymore. I could grow up in my own space and not have to look over my shoulder to see if I would get attacked again.

Sunshine started to shine like the blooming of a flower. Even though we weren't in the best of neighborhoods, our lives only went up from there. My mother was able to make some friends, and it seemed that her decision was good; she could step out independently, and I had my own room.

As my mother started adventuring to figure out some things about herself, she began hanging out with some of our neighbors. After some time, my mother developed the same social knack as my grandparents, effectively communicating with those around her and letting people stay in our house. While not perfect, she did pick up on my grandparents' generosity. Being social and making friends benefited her when she needed a babysitter.

This also netted her a boyfriend, whom she let live in our house. When my mother hung out with her friend, he became our new babysitter. He liked to watch television often; the only TV in the house was in my mother's room.

Then, he would make us go to bed while he stayed in my mother's room. One particular night, he asked me to join him. That air, that drop of dusk, encompassed the room again like before. That paralyzing mist grabbed a hold of me before the man ever did. In the quiet of the night, when no one could hear me cry, he picked me up and forced me on top of him. He only stopped if he heard someone coming.

Once he felt satisfied, he would send me to my room like some servant girl so he could finish watching television.

I remembered pulling my covers over my head, curling up in the bed, hoping the covers would provide enough comfort to help me go to sleep. I didn't know God then, but I sure wished I did. The things I would have said; I just wanted someone to talk to—anyone. Instead, I still heard the same thing. A lurking threat is: "If you say anything to your family, you won't see them again."

Once again, I could not say anything about what was happening to me. For as long as he was living there, he would try to force himself on me.

The physical pain was terrible, but the isolation – it was a different demon. It caused me to feel like I was in this dark place where a stronghold, something unknown, was controlling me. It is hard to explain, and I would never wish this on anyone, not even my enemies.

If I could have talked to someone about it, maybe it would have been bearable, but the silence and the attacks started to eat away at my soul.

An ungodly amount of wrath began to grow in me. I wanted to scream, but all my pain muted it. The molestation, the isolation, and the anger continued to open doors for other problems in my life. Any path I tried to walk in a positive direction led me to a dead end as if walking through a maze. My life became more and more challenging to navigate. I couldn't wait to "get older," as most people would say about tackling problems, but until then, life forced me into a compromising state.

The damaged doors that open in our lives may not be our fault; many times, it is because of the people around us. As I said before, anger and isolation overtook me even at a young age. Those two things affected my decisions, the company I sought, and almost every other aspect of my life.

I could hide from the problems by moving away, but a physical location does not guarantee blessings when open doors are manifested so negatively.

Doors open, and lives become a maze filled with dead-ends, false hopes, and near-endless openings.

Chapter 2

The Maze Begins

Some people might think that the next part of my life would be filled with avoidance: the absolute avoidance of men, of sexual encounters, and of leaving my home, but those people would be wrong.

When we moved, I thought I would be okay, a normal girl living as she should have been. Around nine years of age, we had a neighbor who lived across from us, and as we played together outside, my mother would sometimes let me go over to her house. She was around my age if not some months or maybe a year or two older. She had a bedroom with a kitchen play set, which came with a stove, sink, and refrigerator. She always wanted to play "House," and I had never played that before, but since I wanted to have a friend, I agreed to playhouse with her. I didn't have close friends growing up, especially those I could confide in.

I convinced myself this seemed normal. Being the only girl in a group of boys (brothers, cousins, uncles), playing House seemed new. I usually played sports, climbed trees, and wrestled—the fun stuff. But I was feeling dejected and rejected. No one seemed to notice how I was feeling, and quite frankly, I could use a friend who didn't make me feel so alone. So, I decided to try it. But then something felt wrong about playing this—not in the "it felt different" way, but in the "something was wrong" way. See, this "House" had us playing a married couple, one of us being the father and the other the mother.

At first, was it normal? It then transformed into her trying to kiss me and fondle me. I knew something was wrong here, but she was my new friend, so maybe this was normal? I tried to rationalize it because it was a new experience. However, it kept reminding me of my previous experiences. I didn't wish to continue playing house anymore. Here, another door opens.

These spirals of sexual encounters marked me as a sexually active child, and with that said, I was a mess at a very young age. I began to seek out these experiences with a craving that couldn't be satisfied. Each encounter just made me want to seek another. The same people I should be avoiding became magnets; I was drawn to them. Eventually, these encounters bore fruit.

At the age of 13, another door opened, and I became pregnant. Like most mothers, when she found out, she was furious. She could barely sustain my brothers and me, and now she had to take care of a grandbaby. My mother received government funds and food stamps, but we often had no food. She would work a part-time position at night, but it still wasn't enough to support her family. My brothers and I didn't receive any aid from our fathers (because they weren't around and apparently no enforcement of child support). My two (2) oldest brothers' father were killed in a car accident when they were very young. My mother couldn't do it; she refused to do it, so she told me to get an abortion. That word forever stained my soul as something evil. To my mother, of course, it made sense; she was getting rid of another expense, but it was so much different for me.

I was still a burning city. No one came to douse the flames that formed under their watch. I must admit, I thought having a child who would love and rely on me would be the greatest joy of my life. How could I get rid of that? My mother ignored me for men. My father was nowhere to be seen, and my grandparents were far away. I was at a loss for where to turn.

I started to feel more rage. "If my mother loved and protected me better, maybe I wouldn't need a child to love me in the first place," I thought. "She was incapable of love, or perhaps she hated my father so much that she decided to take it out on me," I thought. The temptation to rebel against her wishes became overwhelming.

"I could do a better job as a mother than she ever was," I told myself. Ultimately, I realized I couldn't care for my child and that my mother was right. She convinced me I could not care for anyone, including myself. I was young, I couldn't get a sustainable job, I couldn't own a home, and without my mother's help, I couldn't be a good mother. So, I took her advice and got my first abortion. The path of thinking started to go somewhere, an easy out for the maze that's been my life – but of course, it wouldn't be that easy.

Without the baby, I could carry the favor of my mother. I decided to work summer jobs when I was 13. I worked to buy my brothers' clothes and shoes for the summer and ensured we had food in the house. The minimum wage was so low that I had to be smart with my money. I saved what I could to get bus tokens until my next payday. I thought this would be sustainable and maybe, just maybe, my mother would pay more attention to me. However, summer jobs didn't last, and the money wasn't enough to help. Back to square one: isolation. It didn't help either that Christmas time was a reminder of my isolation.

My mother would tell me that she only got things for my brothers because that was all she could afford. She assumed that I would understand since I was the oldest. I wouldn't get a single present under the tree during those times. I thought that even if she had bought one thing for all 4 of us, no one would have been left out, but she didn't think of that, or maybe she didn't care.

The isolation in my heart only grew after that. It seemed as though I was attracted to those who only wanted to have sex with me, which opened yet another door. Another door led me to continue looking for more guys to fill my lack of companionship. I sought out more sex partners, one being my neighbor who directly lived next door. He asked me for sex one day, and I couldn't deny the opportunity. This resulted in another pregnancy, not far after my first one.

I had another child. The temptation to keep the child wasn't as strong as the first time. I measured my desire to keep the child with the person who got me pregnant. I felt no love from the boy who got me pregnant. He just wanted a good time, and he got it.

All those sexual encounters had a purpose. They were intended to fulfill a dream. A dream I had was to find someone to love and to find someone who would create a perfect little child with me, and we could become our own family.

Some people don't know why others would settle for a life of constant sex, especially when everyone seems to be doing it for themselves. I did it because I thought it would form the connection I'd been craving for so long. Instead, I know now, it came from the door that was opened when I was molested.

There were times when I would daydream about a better life. A life where I had a mother and a father in the house who loved me, a life where I wasn't molested and could be the child I was supposed to be, a life where I found that perfect person who wanted me for me and not my body. It wasn't my life. I knew it wasn't my life because I couldn't force my mother to love me. My father wasn't a part of my life; I believe I wanted to find that man who would create a perfect baby with me to fill that void.

I also didn't keep the second baby. It didn't feel right, but I kept searching, hoping to fill that void.

Those constant sexual relationships opened another door, this one more physical. During some of my sexual encounters, I contracted gonorrhea. One time, I didn't know I had it, so when the pain started to increase, I was rushed to the hospital and put on around-the-clock antibiotics. The pain felt so much more different than anything I had felt before; among my painful experiences were the high temperatures and the pain in my right side. I had to get emergency surgery as a result of a ruptured appendix.

While resting in the bed, I had to ask myself, "Why was my life like this?" It was truly an understatement to say that my life was not going well. I didn't have direction, I didn't have purpose, and I didn't have love. My lifestyle was a mural of pain. With every new experience, another dreadful picture. I had to do something but didn't know what to do. The paths within the maze stretched long and thin, and the minute I thought I found an opening, it led to another dead-end.

I lived this lifestyle for many years, and these problems followed me well into middle school. As a result, many other things manifested in my pursuit of love. I started playing hooky at school. I paid little attention to the tutor who came to my house, and friction began to appear between my family and me. I was delayed for graduation because of poor attendance and ignoring the work given to me. I felt like I couldn't do anything right.

Once again, changing my physical location would help me improve myself. Living with my mother caused too many problems, so I felt that my grandparents would be a safer place to live. When I lived with my mother, I could see that my grandparents were far superior guardians because they were very strict about getting an education. My aunts, uncles, and cousins were practically glowing; they even had clothes to wear and food in the house. I thought my grandparents would give me the push I needed to take back my life from my bad choices.

I couldn't find the words to describe the feeling of being in that house again. My grandparents had not moved since the time I was molested, meaning that they were still living in the same house where all my troubles began. I was older now, and Malcolm was long gone; I had to see that place as a new beginning, a new door. However, I did reminisce that I wouldn't need a new beginning if the old one was perfect in the first place.

I did see some improvement in my life. My grandparents were much more attentive to my education. I attended school daily, studied, and raised my GPA to 3.63. I even ran for Homecoming Queen and won. Living with my grandparents became one of the first good decisions I made in a long time; it felt right.

To focus better, I kept to myself for the most part, trying to limit my interactions with anyone who seemed to be a negative influence. I wanted to continue at this steady pace and finally take my life back. I began working again to save money for myself and my brothers.

Everything was going so well for me this time. I finally felt like I lifted the curse off my life and would continue to be successful. So, I tried to give love a chance just one more time. Another door was opening.

At work, there was another guy I came to fancy. I told myself I was more mature now; I could handle whatever comes my way. Life was going so well; why wouldn't it? He would come over to my grandparents' house, and we would talk a lot.

Everything was working well: a budding relationship, a job, good grades, and living with my grandparents, who greatly loved me. It was the opposite of my life for the past couple of years. I was convinced he would be the best part of my life until now. So, like everyone who believes they're walking on cloud nine, I decided to push the envelope. Immaturity got the better of me, and I decided to speed up my relationship. I thought love was on my side and had nothing to fear. I opened another door. I slept with him, hoping that this was my chance to reverse my curse completely. Instead, it played like some dark comedy with an imp cackling behind a door.

The relationship started to fade, and he didn't want me anymore. Once again, the long winding path of the maze led to a dead-end filled with thorns. Another physical ailment meant I had to be tested for gonorrhea again; once again, I felt like my life was falling apart. I was convinced no one wanted me; I felt used, abused, and then thrown away. Then the dominoes began to fall...

The only fortunate thing was that my grandparents were able to help me get through high school; they were the motivation I needed. I only wished that their influence could have helped my love life. I couldn't help but feel like I was destined to be delayed—delayed for work, delayed for school, and delayed for love.

Chapter 3

First Love and Broken Curses

Not long after I graduated from high school, I was at a loss for what to do. I struggled to get my diploma, so I became a Nurse's Aide and attended their training courses. I wanted to help people, which was a fine way to do it, but I wasn't altruistic. I couldn't afford college, and that was the easiest way I could take to make something of myself. Though I graduated from the program with an A-, I was no longer interested in that line of work. I decided to work in a department store instead.

In times of silence, I had to figure out my life and what I needed to change to reach that goal that I had set for myself. I was still in a place where I didn't know God, and everything required a physical answer. I was most desperate at these moments, yet I had no answers. My life felt like a record on a constant repeat; regardless of age and location, something happened repeatedly with no change in sight.

I moved back to my mother's house at this time. I didn't see the point of burdening my grandparents further. Their main job was to get me through school, and they did that just fine. I faced a different battle because I decided to move back with my mother.

Working in the department store was nothing to write about; it was a job like any other. I tried to manage my expectations about life because I was often disappointed, and this job was no different. At this point in my life, I knew there had to be some dark blanket lingering over me.

Even when I succeeded, I failed later; when I failed, I would fail so hard that success didn't matter. I would move up slowly in the world, but not enough to be called progress. Everything I did just kept turning around for my bad rather than good.

One day, when I was working, I met a young man around my age who walked in. Let's call him Eddy. He was the son of one of my coworkers. I had already cautioned myself against relationships, but my desire to be with someone overrode a lot of my common sense at that age. I talked with him for a bit, and I tried to take it as slowly as possible. Every relationship I had was never slow, so I didn't have a reference for what "slow" was. But this one was a different one; I felt it.

A part of his appeal was the support I had from his mother; she was so sweet and cared for me like a daughter. With my mother and I developing friction over the years, this was a breath of fresh air to find someone willing to look out for me.

I decided to give this man a shot and see if I could truly find happiness. The two of us would talk on the phone for hours, and I would even visit him at his job, and he would visit me at mine. Our conversations were enlightening and lively as if he understood me. I decided to lay down my guard once again, and after a few days, I felt comfortable sleeping with him. Another door opened, and of course, I became pregnant again. I waited with bated breath to see if his opinions of me would change, but they didn't. Instead, he was overjoyed that we were going to have a daughter, and even his mother was thrilled. She bought everything the baby needed, including the crib. I was genuinely speechless. Was I finally getting my happy ending? One where I could also keep the child and the father involved?

It easily felt like the greatest moment of my life. Maybe this was the reward for such a hard life; my vigilance for love seemed a boon.

Problems did arise. As I got close to my due date, I was hospitalized for asthma, and being pregnant with asthma had its fair share of problems. Eventually, I wasn't alone; Eddy visited me every day and stayed by my side until I could leave. Later in my years, as I grew in the Word of God, He spoke to me and let me know that I was healed from asthma.

Before I was due, I went into premature labor. I had to have a C-section procedure; my baby was born prematurely. Words couldn't describe how enthused I was when my baby was born. Every trial, every heartbreak, and all the pain I felt was worth it when I stared into my baby's beautiful eyes for the first time. "I can do this," I told myself. "I can be a mother." The opportunity presented itself in front of me, and I couldn't believe that, finally, I could have a baby that would love me, like the love I had been looking for. I wasn't alone; no, I had help. I had a loving man and his mother, who loved me. I couldn't believe how blessed I was to have people in my corner—people who loved me unconditionally.

Eddy's mother and I were close; however, she didn't know what I had gone through. She cared for the baby and me and provided everything we needed. Besides, as my child's grandmother, she truly felt like something I didn't have—a friend.

I didn't want to ruin our friendship; if I told her about my past, I felt she wouldn't want to be my friend anymore. Despite my fears, she continued to be a rock in my life. She had suspicions about my life; honestly, I couldn't beat her intuition, but she never pried, and I was forever grateful for her closeness after such trying times. My previous pregnancies resulted in not only the men not wanting anything to do with me but also their mothers not wanting to be involved. Many would look at me scornfully, and it was so hurtful to be judged in such a way.

After my little daughter was born, her father started talking to me about marriage. The mere thought of that nearly brought tears to my eyes. I could easily picture it: staying home with a beautiful child, talking with a mother-in-law who already loved me so dearly. As a vision of my husband walking through the door every day after work. My dream of a loving family was finally in my grasp. I could use this to replace the heartache and the pain in my life. My hatred would turn to love, my hurt would turn to healing, and my turmoil would finally be at peace.

We would talk about the prospect of marriage so often that I spent an enormous amount of time dreaming about it. I customized my wedding dress in my head, heard the bells ringing, and even prepared my guest list.

I would bring these up with him, but I noticed he wasn't as excited as I was. I chalked it up to him being nervous. Of course, this was a commitment, but he loved me. We already had a beautiful child, and his mother fully approved. I wouldn't leave him for anyone else, so I didn't get his apprehension. "Money," I thought; he could be concerned about money. But again, his mother was far more willing to help us out when she could even in the tough times. So, I didn't understand.

Soon enough, however, I would hear less and less from him, almost as if he was fading from the world. I suppose he was fading; he was fading from my world. I wanted to take this up with his mother, but I didn't want to cause any problems; maybe he was planning something that required the utmost secrecy. However, I was wrong. Later, I found out – that he was seeing another woman. The anger that I thought would go away came back; this time, it brought a deep sadness with it as well. Shockingly enough, the girl he was seeing also had gonorrhea. I had to be treated again.

Another door opens, and there goes my happy ending. All those daydreams faded like the evening sun. The pain almost became nostalgic at this point. It returned every once in a while, so familiar and distant at the same time. I wish I could've been immune to the disappointment. The part of me that hoped was the only one that felt the pain. On the other hand, the other me was berating me for thinking I deserved better than what I was given.

He came back to me later. Once again, I fell for it, and once again, I got pregnant. I didn't keep the baby, though; it became one of a long list of abortions I got. It was an easy way out for me. He didn't want another child as well. The initial rift in our relationship never left, and the tension between us became something akin to what my mother and I had. Arguments and fights started to set fire to my mental paradise, burning every dream to ashes. Soon, we separated, unable to stand each other any longer.

I had to ask myself why I was bothered by that dream repeatedly. My early life was filled with such moments: thinking I found love with everything at its peak, all for it to disappear. No matter how long and winding the maze paths would eventually come to a dead-end. Crying was a norm at this point, and I constantly had to think about my life and prioritize. I had to acknowledge what I could do right and where I went wrong. As much as I loved my daughter, I knew that taking care of her alone would be a struggle, especially with her father out of the picture now. Once again, I had to do something differently.

During my time with Eddy, I took the OPM test and passed, and I applied for a government position. Through some family connections, I was able to get a job in a specific agency. With my new position, I received a starting salary at a GS-2/1 with benefits, which also meant I stopped receiving welfare. Honestly, it felt good to move up and away from dependence.

I moved back with my grandparents temporarily so I could get to and from work while I could also pay someone to take care of my daughter. I also had another reason to be there. . . It was hard to relapse when it came to my cravings for love. Their environment was so serene, and their discipline was strict. I couldn't do what I wanted there, no matter my cravings.

Freedom without discipline only gave me more problems, no matter how controlled I thought I was. I didn't know how to put my flesh under subjection.

Later, I moved back with my mother; it was not because of the more freedom I would have because I truly loved her. When I came back home, my mother was in and out of the hospital again due to what had happened to her from the Pastor she received counseling from, who was a voodoo doctor. Thanks to my job in the government, I could help do more in the house and provide more for my brothers.

While there was still friction between my mother and me, I didn't want my brothers to suffer for it. Now, having the responsibility of taking care of my mother made something rise in me to step up to the plate. I had to make trips to the welfare building to get food stamps so I could put food on the table. I had to turn the gas on because we were boiling water to wash up. I paid what I could from my paycheck but had to keep enough so I could make it to work until I got paid again.

We sometimes used a hot plate to cook our food because the gas was turned off. We persevered through the harsh times.

Taking care of my mother was an interesting experience because even though I should've hated her, I couldn't bring myself to leave her. Deep down, I loved her because she was my mother, but I never understood why she didn't love me. As a mother, I didn't know if what I felt was sympathy or the fact that helping people was in my nature.

The love I showed my daughter, and the love my daughter's grandmother showed me revealed something to me about gifts. Kindness is a gift; we should treasure even the smallest amounts of it. How could I receive such love from others and then not want to show it to another? Besides, despite how she treated me, she treated my brothers well, and I couldn't let them suffer because of my qualms about how I was being treated. It wasn't easy, I assure you, and there were times when I would not hold that same love in my heart, but regardless, I did what I needed to do.

My mother did get better, and I took that as a time to move on. I applied for an apartment, and reviewing whether I qualified for housing took some time. So, I stayed with my mother until I could finally get my own place, a one-bedroom apartment that wasn't too far from her residence. Another door opened and getting to my place felt like another dream. It was under a low-income program, but this place was my place. When it was finally time to move in, my mother made a distinct note telling me I could not return to her house. I cannot answer why she would say that, but after what we had been through, I was glad to move.

Anger rose in me again but soon replaced by apathy; I didn't expect much from her. As I said, I did it for my brothers and to be an excellent example to my daughter; what my mother thought of me was of no concern.

I did move into my place, and it took me a while to get my bearings, but soon, my new life began. Again, this felt like the start of a new chapter, but I couldn't get complacent; I still had some problems. I knew for a fact that something needed to change. Having a daughter and moving into a place gave me a new outlook. One was knowing those who truly loved me, and the other was staying away from those I knew had a problem with me. I was fearful of commitments that would lead me down another dead-end path.

Chapter 4

Strong Family Bonds

I can't say that I was the most mature person in the world, but certain things in life taught me lessons that helped me shape my life into a better one. Additionally, it made the realizations I received later in life make more sense.

Sometimes, understanding is enough for people to take the proper action. Knowing what went wrong and why it was the way it was. In my teen years, specific dots were being connected, and yet I couldn't see the whole picture until it was revealed to me. The pieces were starting to take form, especially in this part of my life.

On the weekends, when I lived in my apartment, my daughter would stay with her grandparents which allowed her to see her father while I would hang out with my brother's female cousin. She spent at least two weekends out of the month and some holidays with them. Since my brothers and I didn't share the same father, our family became much more extended than most.

I digress. When I hung out with my family, we would watch more family and some friends ride their motorcycles across V Street in D.C. I overlooked the danger because I was so entranced by the fun of it.

Looking back on it now, I more than likely would have told them to stop if I had known my cousin was going to be hit and killed.

I became friendly with some of the people we would hang out with I mostly spent time with the cousins of my brothers, but I would have other guests as well. I can't forget when I brought a man home, and my brothers decided to come over that day. Their eyes went directly to this man sitting on my sofa, and they nearly ignored me. They bombarded him with questions about who he was and what he planned on doing. To make it a long story short, they kicked the man out and told him to lose my number, and they threatened him not to come near me again.

I was mad that my brothers were getting involved in my business, but when I thought about it later, that probably would have led to another unneeded relationship. As someone picking up the pieces of her heart, the last thing I needed was another dead end. Another door opening that would lead to breaking my heart again. But I must say, though my brothers could sometimes be a blessing, I was tempted more than once to knock them upside their heads.

My family became a significant part of my life. I was so angry with my mother that sometimes I could not see how beautiful of a family I honestly had. Anger has a way of stealing joy.

My brother's cousin was a joy to be around because she was another girl I could talk to. We'll call her Sheela. I can't say enough about how much family was a blessing because having a good foundation was also important to me.

So, it pained me to hear that one of my brother's best friends was gunned down in the neighborhood. "Shock" couldn't begin to explain even comprehend how I felt. He wasn't just any old friend; he was like a brother to us. The news reverberated throughout the family, and even some people took the news harder than others.

Sheela and her other cousin came to my house not long after that. They were supposed to pick me up before we went to our usual hangout on V Street. Before we could leave, a person came to my apartment – my mother. I hadn't seen much of my mother in those days, and this might've been one of the few times that she stepped into my apartment.

I could barely understand what she was yelling at me for. What she said had nothing to do with me, but she was livid and angry. The two of us got into it, shoving and pushing while screaming at the top of her lungs at me. After a little of that, she ran into my kitchen and got one of my knives. I couldn't shake the paralysis, seeing my mother charging at me with a knife in her hand. Different emotions held me down: fear, confusion, and even some rage. I know that we had our differences, but this? She wailed a sound I never heard before while charging for my head. Before I could mount any defense, Sheela's cousin grabbed my mother's arm, wrenched the knife from her hands, and escorted her out.

This experience was so upsetting that I couldn't be comforted yet. Sheela took me to her house because I couldn't even stand to be in the place where my mother tried to kill me. I could only be grateful that my daughter was not there to witness that or, even worse, be attacked because my mother was angry with me.

I finally returned to my apartment in the morning, but that scene kept replaying in my head. Why would she take that anger out on me? I knew I couldn't escape her wrath if she got angry again. I was blessed to have people to protect me, but what about the next time? Could I survive on my own? I had to calm my nerves, and I needed to think rationally and not in fear. I had to convince myself that my mother's attack was simply a one-time thing.

I found out that she was devasted by the death of my brother's friend, but was that enough for her to attack me? Later in the book, you will find out what caused my mother to be so angry. So much was happening simultaneously, and I couldn't take it anymore; I had to leave.

I quickly found another apartment on Call Pl, SE, Washington, DC, that I rented from a private owner. It had two bedrooms with more space. My daughter had her room, but most of the time, she slept with me. I still was catching public transportation, and my daughter's grandparents would help me out with her. She was registered in school around her grandparents' house, and they would come early in the morning to pick us up and drop me off at the nearest subway. My daughter would stay with them until I got home from work. They were so faithful in helping me with her; I will forever be grateful for that.

Again, the beauty of family. It was hard to believe, at least for me, how many people truly cared about my well-being. For so long, I felt so neglected and blinded by my rage and loneliness. Some people cared and did more than care; they went above and beyond for me and my daughter.

Despite the help I was receiving from them, I needed more money to ensure that I could continue to live a comfortable life with my daughter. More specifically, I needed a car. My daughter's grandparents were already doing so much that I couldn't ask them for car money, so I had a plan (a bad one at that). I took out a loan from a place that charged a lot of interest to purchase some weed, thinking I could flip it into some cash. So, I gave it to someone I thought could help me with that, and after a while, I wondered what was taking him so long to get me my money. He skipped out on me and left me with the debt to pay for the loan I took out.

This decision left me with a horrible stomachache for a few days; I couldn't even go to work. I was already struggling for money, and now I have made it worse, not only for me but for my daughter as well. During these moments, I wondered if I was a good mother and if I would make more terrible decisions like that. One wrong decision didn't determine my character, but one bad decision could put us on the streets.

Another door opens, looking for love in all the wrong places. I was in a vulnerable state at this point, which led to more and more relationships that involved sex but no commitments. Quite frankly, the only men in my life who were not family were guys that I had sex with. Why was I continuing this self-destructive behavior?

A couple of months after they moved here, I noticed drug addicts were hanging around our door in our building. That was a big problem. I couldn't allow my daughter to be raised in such an environment. I decided to move again to find someplace better and safer.

I applied for another 2-bedroom apartment in NE Washington, DC. It was on the first floor, and I only took it because it had bars on the windows. I worked two jobs to pay off some debt and loans and to save some money for a down payment on a desperately needed vehicle. When I found a vehicle that was in my price range, my youngest brother helped me with the down payment.

I still had to pay a car note, but fortunately, I no longer worked in Virginia. I was working in Washington, DC, in a new position with a promotion.

When I did not have to work Friday evenings or Saturdays at my part-time position, my daughter and I would pick up some food, get in bed, eat, and watch television until we fell asleep. We would do many things together, including going to the amusement park. Spending time with my daughter without care or worry truly was a blessing. My young dream stood firm in me: to become a better mother than my own and to be there for my child, who loved me as I loved her. I was maturing and lining up my priorities much better than in the past.

Growing up in lack, I didn't want my daughter to want for anything, and of course, I did what I could do for her. However, some of me still wanted that ideal relationship, for a man to love me as I loved him. But at that moment, my daughter had to take priority. Hopefully, I can keep that commitment alive.

One day, I invited my youngest brother and mother to my house to have dinner with my daughter and me. I tried to remedy the situation with my mother despite what was said and done to me. It wasn't an easy task, but I wanted to try it because I loved her; she was my mother.

While we were sitting down and eating dinner, there was a big shoot-out right outside in the parking lot where we lived. Instinctually, we all went straight to the ground.

Again, I was terrified of the implications that this had for my daughter. I wanted to raise her in a good environment, so I was ready to move again, but I didn't know where to go based on my income. This was not the first time they were shooting around where we lived, but we were on the first floor where bullets could have come through the window. Like all things, the situation started to fade into obscurity. However, moving was still on the back of my mind.

Another door opens! Not too long after the shootout, I had my annual GYN examination. I've been seeing the same doctor since 1984. He entered the room without his assistance, and this time, I assumed she was lagging. He was a doctor that I was familiar with, so I didn't think anything of it. Beforehand, I undressed and put on a gown, ready for the examination.

Instead of doing what he was supposed to do, he began fondling my body while pressing his lips to my chest. After all this time, I still sat idle and froze up. All I could do was tremble and remember the exact words that kept me broken, "Say anything, and you'll never see your family again."

I thought about my daughter, who needed me. The doctor had a syringe on the side of the table in the room; my first thought was that he was going to use it on me. I didn't know what was inside the syringe, but a lot of tormented thoughts kept my body still. No other thoughts could manifest until the doctor fixed his pants and left. Finally, in control, I put my clothes back on and ran out of that room. I didn't stop until I was safe in my car and drove home.

I remember not having any air conditioning in the car then, and the weather outside was scorching, but that didn't matter – I just needed to get home. On my way home, more thoughts started: was something wrong with me? I couldn't maintain a proper relationship, and every man who wanted me just wanted me sexually, some even going so far as assaulting me, like my doctor.

I didn't have my answers yet, but God knows I was desperate for one. My problems never ended, no matter how old I got or how far I moved.

When I got home, I settled in my room, thinking about everything that happened that day and how I would proceed. There was the shooting, the many issues and problems that kept occurring in my life, and now this. I knew something was wrong, and this wasn't the right place for us to live. The doctor had my address and knew how to get to me; the tormenting thoughts and nightmares kept me up for a while.

I talked to an attorney and filed a lawsuit against the doctor. He wanted to settle out of court, and we did.

When I received the settlement for sexual assault by the doctor, I paid off all my bills, and I purchased a three-bedroom and two full-bath condo on the 6th floor in Bladensburg, Maryland. Again, I thought that moving would fix my problems and issues. I always thought that if I got far enough away from everything, these problems and issues wouldn't affect me anymore. It seemed that time couldn't even fix them.

Something nagged at me: moving doesn't change your issue. I had to deal with the deep issues inside of me from the open doors in my life. Yet, I always went against that voice, that urge that pushed me to find a more profound solution. I pushed those thoughts back down and tried to enjoy my present—blissfully unaware of my future.

My daughter and I purchased all new furniture, and my only bills were the mortgage, condo fee, and car insurance. We bought new clothes and shoes, and it was just us. No one is going to hurt us here; it's going to be a fresh start.

Chapter 5

The Second Chosen One

Focus on yourself, no relationships. I would tell myself this every time I found myself feeling lonely, even years later, after the doctor incident and my last move. Finding someone who cared for me was difficult; I was left in a constant state of second-guessing their motives. I wanted the future to look bright, like in the movies, but I was reminded daily that these were just fiction.

I just wanted to work hard for my family, for my daughter, who wasn't so little anymore. I couldn't shake how upset I was, knowing that she was watching me in so many messed up relationships. She had to move so many times, too, all because I couldn't find a safe place for us to be. And, of course, raising her without a father in her life. If trying not to raise her like my mother raised my brothers and me was the goal, I was failing miserably – I could barely see the difference.

To be honest, I was surprised I had a daughter at all. Before I had her, I had to have surgery to have my right fallopian tube removed due to a cyst. My left fallopian tube was blocked from the top to the bottom, and the doctor stated that I could not have any children. Yes, I had my daughter, but I realized I may not have any more children.

Instead of running the maze like I used to, I leaned on the bristle walls, tired of where the journey took me. If thorns were at the end of every road, then what was the point of continuing? There were times when I would find the strength to move through the path of life, and other times when I would sit down and cry. I was always getting the short end of the stick in every relationship, and sometimes, I wouldn't even get the stick.

With so much going on, I started attending my childhood church with my daughter. I wanted to raise her in a better environment. We became regulars, attending the Wednesday service and the Sunday service. It felt good to be around my family, but I didn't truly understand what was happening in that church. I didn't consider myself saved; it was more like I was scared. At this point in my life, church wasn't a lifestyle; it was a false sense of security, a mentality of "nothing bad happens to church people." I wasn't too deep into the Word, but I decided that maybe this could all work out.

As I continued to attend my childhood church, I was told by one of my family members that I should ask the Pastor to bless my condo, so I did, and he agreed to it. He let me know when he would be available to bless my condo and asked me what time my daughter went to bed. I was very skeptical; I thought, why would someone ask that? Maybe he thought it would be too boring for her, or he didn't want to disturb her while blessing the house. I told him the time, thinking he would come before she went to bed, but he came three hours later.

When I let him in, he immediately tried to kiss me; once again, anger rose in me, and history was repeating itself, so I kept my distance from him, especially since my daughter was still awake at the time, and I was so glad that she was still up. Once he saw this, he prayed over the condo and left. I had much to ponder that night. Why? Wasn't he supposed to be better than everyone who tried this before? I didn't know what to make of it, nor did I understand what made me stay in the church. However, it was the only safe place, so I continued attending.

The pastor called me regularly. He was always asking if he could talk to me or come over to see me. I still attended the church, but I started to become overwhelmed. Not only was his constant harassment shaking me, but he was married. One Sunday, his wife sat behind me in church because her husband would always stare at me from the pulpit when he preached. She always glared at me as if she wanted to drag me to the gates of Hell herself. He wanted to sleep with me, did I wear a sign on my back that kept drawing people to want to have sex with me?

I had enough; instead of running, I decided to try something different; I prayed. I told God my woes, and I knew that sleeping with a married man, especially a pastor, was against the Word of God. I may not have been deep inside my word, but I just talked to God as if I were talking to someone else.

I learned a valuable lesson from this: just because we are familiar with a place doesn't mean it was meant for us to stay. I didn't consult God about where I should've been; instead, I made more decisions with my head. Being a Christian doesn't exempt us from making natural decisions; we can easily make our own decisions and then lie to ourselves that God co-signed that decision. When we don't seek God first for guidance, instructions, and directions, He will not authorize our choices and decisions.

I decided to stop attending church because, in the end, I knew it wasn't the best place for me and my child. However, I was still lost and unable to find a way out. I was back to square one again. I was so ignorant of the things of God that I wasn't dedicated in any way. So, I continued to live for two things: myself and my daughter. I hoped that would change things for the better.

I had the heart of a fighter, so I chose to keep going, even though the path would be a dead end. I only needed to be right once, and my future would be set. I continued to work in my new job, and the promotion did my daughter and me well. Since it was just the two of us, I could pamper her in ways I could have only dreamed of when she was born.

Another door opens! Maybe I pampered us too much because I started to attract someone's attention. I worked in the same office with a military man (who we'll call Calvin), who eventually became very kind to me. I tried to keep my distance, but every moment I saw him, something in me wanted to give him a chance. From the relationships that amounted to something to those that didn't, I always assumed the new person was different. This one was no different in the end.

Once we started to get to know each other, I would have him come over and listen to a lot of romantic and jazz music. His music taste drew me to him. I didn't know that he was already involved with someone else then. I opened the door for him to leave her and move in with me. I shared my lawsuit with him and briefly told him what I went through with the doctor. He was with me because he knew I had money; in his mind, he was using me to get what he could from me. Once again, wrong choices and decisions.

As all these relationships went, we eventually started having sexual relations. With my surgery, I didn't have to worry about being pregnant, but I didn't think about protected sex because I didn't think he didn't look like he would have an STD, so I saw this as an opportunity to have unprotected sex with him.

He would buy me flowers and other lovely things, including a watch, which I had never received from anyone else before. Our relationship was steady, with no significant moves on either side. But something unexpected happened—I got pregnant.

We were amazed because I wasn't supposed to have children anymore. Even the doctors were shocked by such a development. Honestly, I couldn't be happier. My dream to have a child with someone I loved hadn't faded into dust. I truly felt like this was the moment I was waiting for.

They told me I would have a son, and like my daughter, he would be celebrated as a beautiful addition to our family. This seems to be working out. Everything fell into place and was much more accessible than in all my other relationships. It seemed too good to be true, but Calvin genuinely loved me. He gave me a wonderful and handsome son and my daughter gained a little brother.

He wanted our relationship to be something tangible, so he finally asked me something I've always wanted to hear – "Will you marry me?" He wanted to marry me. He wanted to marry me! He told me that I would get benefits for being married to him and would even be able to use the military facilities as a military wife. He wanted to ensure we were cared for even in his absence.

I honestly couldn't believe it. I was in awe. Finally! A dream come true: someone who loved me and wanted a family! And commitment, he wanted commitment! Of course, I said yes to him, and we were eventually married. He came through on his promises, and we got the help we needed. It felt so good to finally be married and in a solid relationship. I wanted to give everything I had to make this work.

Since he was doing his part, I decided to do mine. When he needed transportation, I helped him get a vehicle to get back and forth from work. Once I shared with him about the lawsuit, he married me so he could get a car and have his transportation.

However, after a few months in our relationship, I noticed the love leave his eyes. He wasn't as energetic as he once was to see me, nor did he bother to do what we did when we were dating.

One day, he came home, and he started fighting me, dragging me on the carpet. I had developed bad burns, and he would hit me in the face to the point where I would develop knots. I didn't know what came over him, but it became a routine.

In other fights, he began choking me, telling me that he was going to make my life a miserable one. I wanted to fight back, but I was still pregnant with our son at this time, and I would rather spend time protecting my son than fighting my husband. Some nights, when he wouldn't abuse me, he would go out at night and leave me in the house, not returning until morning.

I didn't get it. I waited and waited for the right man. I did everything I needed to be a perfect wife, and this is what I got. It was like living with my first abuser all over again; I just had to wait for the terror to descend, and I couldn't defend myself when it did. The stress was something I had a hard time dealing with, especially since I was pregnant.

However, things started to calm down, and I thought I could catch a breather. My daughter's uncle had gotten someone pregnant around this time. She and I would talk sometimes on the phone. So, though we were not friends, we had a common association and were both in similar situations, so we decided to hang out. One particular time, she wanted to see the condo I had just purchased, so I showed her around. It was a quick visit, so I returned to the complex, left my hazard lights on, and continued to the condo.

When we returned downstairs, we tried to enter the car, but someone else was around, too. There was a man in the shadows of the building. He wore gloves and followed my acquaintance and me to the car. As soon as we tried to enter, he attempted to hold the door open, trying to force us out of the car and steal it. Fortunately, we were already inside, so I managed to speed off before he could force one of us out.

To this day, I am grateful to God for getting us out of that situation safely. And I was grateful for the fact that even after all that, the stress didn't affect the birth of my son.

Now, at the time of my due date, I was constantly going back and forth to the hospital because of physical abuse from my husband. This one particular time when I went to the hospital, the Commander from Andrews Air Force Base in Maryland put me in the hospital because she knew that I was being abused. I was able to stay in the hospital until my son was born.

My son was another miracle child born to me even when I thought I could not have children. I loved looking at his smiling face, but I had to think about the situation he was born into. His mother had a lot going on and couldn't keep it together, and his father was abusive; how could he grow up in such circumstances? I had to try my best, but I wasn't sure what my best could do.

Within that week, when we were discharged from the hospital, my husband wasn't home that day, so I used it as an opportunity to get my son acclimated to his new home. Also, my daughter had a new role as an older sister, something I'm all too familiar with.

When Calvin finally returned home, he came into the house angry and started yelling accusatory things at me as if I had been cheating on him. He then went into my bag and started sifting through it, expecting to find a number or some other piece of evidence.

He began doing what he usually did; he started pushing me and throwing me around while I was holding our son. I instinctively went to protect my stomach, but then I realized – I wasn't pregnant anymore. I gave our son to my daughter and asked her to forgive me for the violence she was about to see. While I do not condone violence now, enough is enough.

A winning battle or a losing one, I didn't care; I decided to fight back. After that altercation, he decided to call the police to sway them to his side. However, when I was pregnant, I would call the police because of the domestic violence that I was experiencing from my husband, and the police were at our home constantly. They were, unfortunately, familiar with us at this point.

Upon their arrival, he tried to convince them that I was the one instigating these violent instances, but instead of believing him, they laughed at him.

They were all too aware of his behavior and his treatment towards me, especially since I had been calling them since the start of my pregnancy. So, after taking a report, they left. He then tried to call my daughter's grandmother (who was still in my life, thank God) and wanted to get her to his side. Calvin would tell her that I went crazy and that she should come and see about me. So, like any responsible woman would do, she rushed over. When she got there, however, I made sure to set the record straight about what was happening. She found out that my husband had been putting his hands on me, but she was surprised because usually, when her son would fight me, I fought him back, sending him home with a busted lip and/or nosebleed. She was surprised it took me a long time to fight back.

After the altercation with the police, the visit with my daughter's grandmother, and, of course, the fact that I wasn't going to sit around and let him hit me, he stopped physically abusing me. Maybe it didn't give him the same thrill as it used to. He wasn't done with me, though; he still tried to abuse me verbally, probably in an attempt to break my will so I would stop fighting back.

He constantly told me he needed his space, so he would stay out every other night, never bothering to return home or call. Another woman would call the house asking for him, and I figured that he was cheating on me anyway. To further cement my theory, the days we weren't fighting, we would engage in sexual relations, and he would call me another woman's name. I confronted him about it, but he denied it. His unfaithfulness caused me to be diagnosed with genital herpes, an STD an incurable disease. (When I gave my life to Jesus Christ and learned that He was a healer, I started taking the Word of God as my medicine, and I received my healing and was made whole; in the name Lord Jesus Christ, so be it. Jesus is the Healer.)

I surmised that the reason he kept trying to accuse me of cheating was so that he could hide his actions. I knew he was bad news, but I still decided to make things work, hoping he would change. The verbal abuse didn't stop. He started attacking how I was in bed and introduced me to pornographic movies in hopes that I would get better for him. It didn't pan out the way he wanted, so he stopped trying to force them on me.

Our marriage became a pattern of highs and lows, abuse and berating comments, then things mellowed out, and we would be a happy family again. "Happy" meant not fighting in my case.

The days of non-abuse would be him leaving and not returning. Eventually, he told me to leave the military housing and find a new place for the kids and me to live. At that point in my life, I didn't know what to do. The condo was rented out. I was just confused, bruised emotionally from my past experiences, and bruised physically and emotionally from my current relationship. Another path in the maze that led to nowhere fast. You would think I would have given up already with how many things went wrong. For once, I wanted some relief, not something that would appear suitable but truly good. And what I found didn't come without its own set of challenges.

Chapter 6

Salvation

When my husband told me to leave the base with the children, I was at a complete loss for what I needed to do. To add insult to injury, my funds from the lawsuit were depleted. Back to the start of the maze, this time with another child and again with no one to love. It was the love that I had for my children that kept me moving forward. I journeyed back to Maryland, finding an apartment there and hoping to make sense of things. Life wasn't fair sometimes. It always felt like something was out there waiting to seduce me with promises of a happy life and then tear me down.

I knew something had to change, but I didn't exactly know what. I tried everything I could have possibly tried, and look where it got me. So, I resorted to something that I hadn't done in a long time, I prayed.

I asked God to reveal Himself; I wanted to know this true and living God. I didn't like what the Pastor at my childhood church advertised or the God that people slapped on their bumper stickers. I wanted someone who could save me and provide me with relief.

Another door opened! I was sitting down at my dining room table contemplating suicide –I couldn't take it anymore. Then, I heard a voice as loud as someone beside me say, "In order to come to the

Father, you have to come through the Son, the Lord Jesus Christ." I was in awe.

God spoke to me, someone who ignored his word for a long time. I returned to the Word, hoping to get more of God in my life. I wanted to open the door for him to move into my life. And that's precisely what happened.

There was a young lady where I worked who ministered the word of God to me every chance she got, and it was so real that I desired more of it. As she and her fiancé continued to minister the Word of God to me, I felt a stronger pull to the message of God. They noticed this and invited me to their church. Before I could join them, however, I had to inform them of what happened to me with the pastor before. After all, that is why I left church in the first place.

My coworker assured me that no such thing would happen because their pastor was a woman, and she was the one teaching on Sunday at 11 a.m.

After a little more convincing, I gave church another shot. I took my children with me, and we attended church service the next Sunday.

When we arrived, the congregation was in the middle of praise and worship. I can only recall the serenity of the atmosphere; it honestly felt like nothing I had felt before. The sweetest breeze near the bluest ocean couldn't compare to it. Before we could sit down, the congregation began to lift their hands high in the air and speak in a language I had never heard of before.

After that experience, I kept attending church. I honestly didn't know if I was growing spiritually then, but something about the messages began clicking within me. I even started attending classes, although I didn't have the funds to pay for them. However, the Lord provided for me with every class I took.

I learned the importance of paying tithes and offerings, the power of God's blessing over my finances, and how to give. I truly felt like I was growing as a person. I got into my word increasingly, which didn't feel inconvenient.

Everything went right, and for the first time, I truly felt like I was growing meaningfully. I learned about the spiritual principles that defined my life, and so many questions were answered.

Another door opened! Everything seemed to be going in the right direction. Then something even more miraculous happened. Calvin called me, saying that he wanted to do the right thing. I couldn't believe it; I allowed him in my life again, hoping things would change. I set the ground rules almost immediately: we had to go to counseling with the pastor and restart this marriage on the right foot instead of stumbling through it. He agreed, and we began counseling as soon as we were able. Everything was working well; it felt like he was listening to the counseling and making the proper changes.

He also enrolled in Bible College, and the two of us began taking classes together. He seemed like a different man. I don't know what happened to him after we moved away, but he became a much better husband and father.

I just had to thank God; this had to be the Lord's doing. The man I love has finally returned to his senses and is not the abusive man he was to me before. This was the person I married. His new behavior even sparked something in our love life, and I managed to get pregnant again. Another miracle topped off with another miracle. I thought my son was supposed to be the last child, but now I would have another.

When I went to the hospital for the sonogram, I found out that I wasn't going to have just one child; I was going to have two! Twins! Birthed to me at the point of my rejuvenation. I must've won the spiritual lottery with how much God had blessed me. This was the moment I'd been waiting for when I finally left the maze and found my true path with someone I love at my side.

After a couple of months, I started having such painful cramps and spotting that I had to make an appointment to see the doctor. I was already preparing my two children for two more. Especially my son, who's the youngest, and how I would need him to help me with his two youngest siblings.

Anyway, when I went to the doctor, I was kept in the hospital for some time, longer than usual. Upon his return, the doctor looked somber, and I had to ask what was wrong.

Of course, I knew what was wrong; it was apparent. But sometimes, it's not until the words hit you that you understand what they truly mean. When the doctor opened his mouth, it took me a moment to sit back and process it all. I was threatening a miscarriage.

No more twins.

Moments like these, me think about my life. All those abortions I had. How I took the life of my children for granted. When I wanted a baby, it was taken from me.

I had to break the news to my family, and news like that is never easy. However, it almost became overshadowed by Calvin's deployment to South Korea. Soon, our family had to be separated. In such a trying time, I wanted someone to lean on, but when duty calls, someone must answer.

Before he was deployed, he got us military housing again so we could live on the post. After a year, he returned. It felt good to be reunited at last. Although my children were older, I still held onto my faith.

Not too long after his return, I started to get cramps, and they grew increasingly worse as time went on. So, I decided to go to the hospital, and my husband accompanied me. After a few tests, the doctor said that I had chlamydia.

I had been faithful at home with the children, keeping up with my faith. He, on the other hand, was in a foreign country. So, naturally, I decided to look at him. Like a fervent prayer warrior, he shouted in his lungs that it wasn't him, and he denied it in front of me and the doctor. It was not until the doctor silenced him with the facts that he realized that my husband was the cause.

I was hurt, yes, but this is not something I haven't seen before. This was the version of him who would leave all night and not return until morning. Days after that were almost strewn together. I had difficulty forgiving him, and I couldn't continue this anymore.

The pain truly set in when all these women started calling the house. One woman called my house telling me she had a baby daughter and that Calvin was the father. I confronted him about it, and he first denied that she was his daughter. Later, he pleaded with me, saying that a little girl was born before he tried to get his life together. This was all before he changed.

A part of me wanted to believe his story so I wouldn't sabotage my chances at a happy marriage. Another part of me wanted to leave him just as he left me. It was a moment that left me without words to pray. He seemed so genuine when he tried to convince me, but the news of his daughter, coupled with the chlamydia, truly felt like he didn't mean what he said.

Maybe it was a false sense of faith or naiveté, but I eventually forgave him and decided to work on our relationship. Another open door! Later, he received orders to be stationed at Lawton, OK. He wanted all of us to come with him. He thought it would be a place for a fresh start, no lies, no cheating, no backbiting.

A new environment meant things would change. How many times have I told myself that lie? While packing for the move, I heard God's voice again: "Your husband is planning on taking you there to abandon you." I immediately rebuked the voice. Why would my husband do that after being so sincere? Maybe my doubts manifested into a voice, or the devil tried to make me not fight for my marriage. I ignored the voice of the Holy Spirit when He was warning me.

We eventually moved, and I had to trust God for a job in the federal government. Until I was approved, I had to be a stay-at-home mom for a bit, which allowed me to help my daughter get ready for school and take care of my son, who was not school age yet.

This also helped me stay in the Word much more effortlessly. While working around the house, I listened to the CDs I received from Jericho City of Praise and Kenneth Copeland Ministries. I had faith in my position and eventually got the job I applied for. We also enrolled our son in a Christian School since he was too young to attend public school.

A few months had passed since our move. While life seemed normal enough, I was still thinking about the voice I heard before we left. Sometimes, I would look at him at night, wondering what he was thinking about me and my family. Would he abandon us at such a time? Fear of loneliness and abandonment crossed my mind frequently, those feelings so familiar in my life.

Not too long after that, I became pregnant again. I wondered how I would so easily become pregnant after being told in the past by the doctors that the chances were so slim. It was not too long into the pregnancy that I started to feel pain, and I started to bleed. I realized that I was threatening a miscarriage. I had to be rushed to the hospital, where the doctor told me exactly what I was thinking. Not again. I told myself.

I cried out to God that day; I was tired of how my life was a constant string of disappointments and miscarriages. I told Him that I wanted my baby to live, and I decided in my heart that I wasn't going to lose another one, not again. I did everything I could to keep myself and my baby safe.

I was on bed rest until the bleeding stopped, and I was able to return to work. There were some complications after that, but it seemed that my baby was going to live. I found out that I was going to have another little girl. A precious gift from God in the midst of my uncertainty.

It was nearly time for her to be born, and after many trials and tribulations, I could see her beautiful face. During my entire pregnancy, I spent so much time with God because I believed no one else could save me from the heartache of another miscarriage. I needed God's grace and mercy.

Things were looking up for Calvin, too. Fortunately, he left the military and got a new job. The downside was that his new position required him to travel to Winston-Salem, North Carolina. I was happy for him; I believed a new position would solidify our fresh start! Maybe that voice was wrong after all; this seemed like a great opportunity for our family. I still had my insecurities, but who wouldn't, after all I had been through?

One night, before he left for his trip, I was upstairs when I heard a woman's voice downstairs. I thought everyone was asleep, so I was curious. I tip-toed down the stairs and saw my husband on the computer, talking to some woman. It was not a familiar voice, so I investigated further. Upon a quick inspection, I realized what was going on – my husband was into pornography. He was talking to some porn star. I snuck back upstairs and immediately felt that painful heartache I often experienced. Could this really be happening?

The next day, he eventually left for Winston-Salem, North Carolina, and I didn't have the courage to tell him what I heard. I wanted to believe that maybe I misunderstood, but I knew what I heard. He said he would change; maybe I wasn't trusting him enough. But my trust was broken so often that I automatically leaned toward expecting the worst.

I tried to ignore my doubts and go about my life like normal. During my pregnancy with my youngest daughter, I thoroughly enjoyed breakfast food with a side of chocolate cake, a habit I kept up even after her birth. I ate the heartiest meals one evening before hearing, "Call him." I knew that voice; that was the Holy Spirit. I argued with him and told the Holy Spirit I could trust my husband, but He was insistent, "Call him." Eventually, I relented, and I did.

He never answered his phone, which was confusing because he was staying at a hotel while away. I then tried to reach the front desk. They agreed to check his room, but to no avail; he was not there.

I was worried that something had gone wrong with his trip—perhaps he had been mugged, or something terrible had happened. I didn't want my insecurities to cloud my judgment. I called the police in the area, hoping they could find him and help him if necessary. They began searching the hotel to see if they could find out where he may have gone and to see if anyone had seen him.

The police eventually called me back, and some of me wished they hadn't. They told me my husband was with another woman (I heard him arguing with them in the background). I thanked the officers and hung up the phone. Then I knew why it is so important to be obedient to the voice of the Holy Spirit: He knows all things, even man's hidden secrets and thoughts.

I could only blame myself. I gave this man another chance when I shouldn't have. His empty promises couldn't fix whatever was going wrong within him. Upon his return, things began to deteriorate even more. He started staying out late again, coming home without saying anything. He already abandoned the family mentally, so this was just a manifestation of how he already felt. Fear, loneliness, and now anger and disappointment overwhelmed me.

Due to this stress, I had to go to the hospital because I was having contractions. Fortunately, I was discharged. The next day, I had an appointment where my (oldest) daughter's middle school, and after the conference, she and I decided to spend the rest of the day together.

We also had to make a very difficult decision to take our puppy to the animal shelter. As much as we loved this little puppy, it was all I could do to care for the family. My son really enjoyed playing with the puppy. However, the puppy added an additional cost: as he played with my son, he would bite holes in his clothes. So, I thought it was the best thing to do before the baby was born.

As if part of some movie, when my daughter and I arrived at the shelter, my water broke, and I went into labor. God provided for my family and me. Soon, another family member joined us. The third miracle in a long list of them. (A child I believed would rejuvenate my marriage, and maybe things could be patched up.) Instead, things got worse.

I didn't want to stay anymore; I don't think I had the strength to. It finally clicked with me. I had to surrender. My next prayer was for a clean separation. We would go our separate ways, never to see each other again, and do this for the sake of our children. Our children deserved better. Our home was not a place of serenity.

I vividly remember one morning when I was sifting through the mail. I found something incredibly peculiar—a $1,000,000 life insurance policy with my name on it. Instantly, I panicked. At the time, I had a friend who went to Jericho City of Praise with me, and we talked about this. Everything in my head was moving faster than I could process it. Yet, every thought led to the same conclusion—you need to get out of there.

Since my husband wasn't home, I thought it would be the perfect time to start to pack. I tried to pack as many things as possible so I could leave. I tried to take the crib down, but I needed help. At some point during the packing, the Holy Spirit spoke again, "Put everything back and go to bed." Now, with everything that was going on, I didn't expect that; I expected the Lord to try and deliver me like the Israelites from Egypt. Instead, he gave me a special prayer that, to this day, I still pray, "Lord, fill this house up with the Precious Blood of Jesus and make it so thick that no ungodly spirit can stay here, dwell here, or enter in. In the name of the Lord Jesus Christ, so be it." After that, I went to bed.

My husband stayed out all that night and came home early the next morning wearing a suede jacket. He came upstairs and walked into our bedroom with his hands in his pocket. It was mid-September in Oklahoma, so it was far too hot to be wearing what he was wearing. I remember this moment like it was yesterday. I immediately wondered what he was trying to do, but I decided to stay in bed.

He then demanded that I hand over my wedding rings. I refused, and he stared at me for a long time. I couldn't remember how long it was, but it seemed like a lifetime before he left. I didn't truly process what happened, but I felt confident the Lord protected me from something.

When he returned home that day, he never came to the bedroom; he just stayed on the couch. By God's grace, the following day, the military moved him. Since he was allowed one final move at the military's expense after leaving the Army, that was the last I saw of him. Before he left, he took all the money out of the account except $13.00.

Open doors were such a strange phenomenon to me at the time. Despite their life-changing circumstances, how was it that so many people can base their decisions on narcissism? I realized now that Calvin also had a problem with open doors, one that marrying me couldn't fix.

His narcissistic behavior left no room for me or our family. Neither of us realized doors do not close gently on their own; many times, they are slammed shut.

Most people would have been upset or angry, but all I could feel was peace. I didn't get the happy ending I wanted with him, but in the end, I realized something about myself—and now maybe I can open doors that I truly want to open. I can open doors that lead me to follow God's Word, not my own.

We were still married; however, when he left me, I could go to the military, and they extended my benefits (even though he didn't retire from the military, he just departed when his term was finished). I was able to go to the hospital in Oklahoma to get cases of ready-to-feed bottles of formula, and that was the favor of God. My grandmother paid for a one-way airline ticket for my youngest brother to come and help us get back home. I spent time with God the day after he left. I had unexpected income in my mailbox, and money was wired to me.

I moved back to Maryland and stayed in a hotel at Andrews Air Force Base. God blessed us with an apartment before the Ft. Sill, Oklahoma, human resources office could relocate me to a position in the Virginia, Maryland, and Washington, DC, area. With minimal funds available after the deposit and first month's rent, I had to have Faith to believe God that my new position would soon manifest, and it did. To God be all the Glory!

That was the favor of God. Once settled in our new home, we started attending Jericho City of Praise again.

Chapter 7

What Came After

To take a step back in time before my divorce. Calvin's parents had called me to inform me that he was locked up for owning an illegal gun that he had purchased in Oklahoma. He had it in his pocket when he stood on the side of the bed with his suede jacket on. Do you remember when he took the $1,000,000 life insurance policy out on me and how awkward I felt when he stood staring at me in that suede jacket?

After he moved back to Buffalo, New York, and before he was locked up, we had already moved and settled in our new home back in Maryland. I had to file Chapter 7 because there were bills, including the car he was driving, that I could not afford to pay because my salary dropped over $3,500 a year, and I had to take care of my family.

We were briefly living in our new place before I was led to move again because he was coming into the area looking for us. I spoke with someone in the rental office, and they allowed me to break my lease. I had a condo mentioned in the prior chapters that we moved back to that was included in Chapter 7. He called me when he came into the area with his cousin, arguing because he wanted to see the children. I was not led for us to be around him, and he didn't know where we lived, which was a great thing. I thank God for protecting us. Not too long after he left Maryland, his parents called to tell me he was locked up.

When he was incarcerated, he filed for divorce. After my divorce was finalized, I was so very happy. I had to sort many things out because my own life and my children's lives were now up to me. With so many things on my mind, I felt overwhelmed and wondered if my direction was based on my faith or my sanity.

I have mentioned open doors constantly in this book because they plagued me more than anything else. Unfortunately, if those doors are not closed properly, they could also plague your life, your children, and generations to come. Once we got settled and were back attending church, my co-worker and her husband separated, and he needed a ride to church, so I started picking him up. This was a very bad move—another open door!

This was a year after my youngest daughter was one. This man didn't have any transportation. I felt like I owed him because he and his fiancée at the time used to minister the Word of God to me in a way that I never heard it to be explained that way before. They told me about God the Father, Jesus Christ, and the Holy Spirit, and it was so real that I just wanted to hear more that I would be up on the phone with them after midnight or later.

Sometime later, there was trouble in paradise. The man and his wife had some issues, which led to a divorce. I stayed in contact with the man since he had to move back in with his father, who lived fifteen minutes from my home at the time. My family and I would take him to Sunday service with us, and we would fellowship on the way. I could salvage our little band because the way they spoke about God just moved me.

On my way to church one day, I heard the Voice of God; however, I was still learning His voice. I understood how people in the Bible could be so fearful of a voice they didn't recognize or understand. Regardless of who it was, the word didn't make sense to me, "Don't take that man to church today." It had to be the Devil, I thought. Indeed, God wouldn't tell me not to take someone to church. Besides, I knew this man then; he had to be one of the holiest people I knew. I sought someone else's opinion but didn't know who was speaking. I listened to advice from man and ignored the voice of The Holy Spirit who warned me. How I regret once again taking man's advice, which opened another door.

I am a professional Christian Clown (yes, we exist). I was a clown before I gave my life to Christ, so when I got saved, I took every aspect of myself, including that, and gave it to the Lord. One night, when I was asleep, He came to me in a vision and told me that He wanted me to be a Christian clown, no longer called tricks, but demonstrations based on faith using the Word of God as my foundation. Each demonstration was based on faith scriptures, and the kids got involved. That same Sunday, I ignored the voice of the Holy Spirit. That Sunday, I had to perform at the nursery and sometimes at the children's church during services.

After service, I had to head to the military base since I was separated from my ex-husband, who used to be in the Army. In one of the stores on base, I had a layaway I needed for my children since school was starting. At this time, my oldest daughter would spend the weekend with her father and grandparents, and she wasn't there with us that day. So, I was just with the young man, my youngest daughter, and my son. The young man that the Holy Spirit warned me not to take to church. The Holy Spirit is awesome because He warns us of things to come before they happen, but it is up to us to be obedient to His voice.

Like the Motor Vehicle Administration (or MVA as it's commonly known to have long wait times), it took a long time for them to call my number. While waiting, the man got up and told me he wanted to take my little girl for a stroll. I didn't want to worry about them calling my number and looking for my children after, so I denied the request. I wanted to leave as fast as possible without any issues. I was still in my clown outfit, which grew increasingly uncomfortable by the minute and attracted attention from the nearby people and their children. The transition did not go smoothly because I ignored The Holy Spirit's voice.

They finally called my number as I was going to get my items. The man took my daughter and son for the walk he had previously asked me about. I yelled at him, but he didn't hear me, and I'm sure he did, but he ignored me. I had already told him "No," but he disrespected my answer. I huffed and decided to get my layaway items before tracking them down.

It took them a very long time to find my layaway. After I got the items, he came back with my son and daughter and we left. However, when my daughter returned to me, she was crying profusely. I assumed she was hungry, or maybe she just missed me. So, I planned on dealing with that when we got to the car or home since we were still on base.

Once we were done, we left and managed to drop him off and we went home. After dropping him off, my daughter was still crying; she cried the entire ride. Immediately, I felt that something wasn't normal. I rushed home and took her to our bedroom that we shared together so I could see what was wrong with her. I tried feeding her, but she wasn't hungry, so I changed her diaper.

When I opened the diaper, the usual sight of poop was there, but then I realized – the poop was bloody. Her rectum was swollen as well. A flash of memories started to swell inside of me; I knew for a fact what happened to my daughter, something I was unfortunately familiar with.

I reached for the phone immediately to call the police, but then I heard dark, hazy voices whispering things to me, "They'll call you an unfit mother. They'll take your daughter and all your other children away, and you'll never see your family again." The phone froze in my hand momentarily, but I had enough strength to thaw myself out and at least call someone. I tried calling other people to help me, but no one answered their phone.

I was so angry at the choices and decisions I would make. How could I let this happen to my little girl? How could I be so neglectful?

This was the same type of ignorance my own family had when I went through this pain; now, look at me, committing the same mistake like clockwork.

I just cried that day, crippled and paralyzed by the fear. I didn't even think of taking my daughter to the hospital because of how overwhelmed I was. I just let the day pass without taking any proper action.

The following day, by God's grace, I could move—I could think. A couple assisted me by taking us to the hospital to get my daughter checked out. It was so long ago to recall what the doctor said, but they assured me she was okay. But the image of what took place with my daughter because of my disobedience constantly kept tormenting my mind. I cried not for days but many years. I called him and confronted him. I called him, rage building in my eyes and heart. Of course, he denied it; even in my anger, I knew no one would accept such a harsh allegation. I didn't want to take any more lies or excuses, so I hung up the phone and tended to my daughter.

Later in the day, in a turn of what I assumed was a holy conviction, he called me to admit it and asked me to forgive him. My blood boiled at the thought that he could have the audacity to ask this of me. His actions reminded me of every act that happened to me. I wanted to protect my children from this mess; I didn't want them to experience anything that I went through, but this moment made me feel unfit, unprepared, and unwilling.

I have seen that man's face multiple times after the fact, and I knew I truly never forgave him. I carried on the pain for years, returning to that dark place over and over again. I was tormented by the thoughts of what I should've done. What had happened to my baby girl just kept playing in my mind, and thoughts over and over again, constantly tormented. It felt like – no – a curse of torment formed a haze that trapped my mind. But that was the battle, the mind. What he did was horrible, but the action itself was already finished. I had to forgive him for myself, my daughter, and my future; I couldn't resume giving him power over me.

As I said, this felt like a test of my faith or sanity. However, regardless of what it was, it truly opened my eyes to the impact of open doors and what they could do to myself and my family.

However, despite all this, I know that it is vital for us to love and forgive. I spent most of my life trapped in the cage of unforgiveness and realized I was making the people who hurt me, my gods. They lived in my head, dictated my actions, and had their words echo in my mind. Love and forgiveness are not for the person who did it but for the person who was hurt.

We can't allow people to hold us in bondage by having that kind of power over us, nor can we keep them in bondage if they genuinely wish to change. If they ask God to forgive them, we should also find it in our hearts to forgive them.

The hate, the hurt, the rage, the pain, none of it is worth it. The part of our hearts that we give to the pain should be given to God, who has the power to remove burdens and destroy yokes.

I had to learn to forgive because my Heavenly Father instructed us to do so. He could not forgive me if I didn't, and I desperately needed forgiveness. If He can forgive me for everything I experienced, I can forgive others, and you can forgive me, too.

Chapter 8

Overcoming

Revelation 12:11 "And they overcame him (the devil and his demons) by the blood of the Lamb (Our Lord and Savior Jesus Christ) and by the word of their testimony."

Even though I have given my life to Jesus, attended church, and even a Bible College, I still needed deliverance. I had a lot of past hurt in me: the verbal, physical, mental, and sexual abuse still had their clutches on me because I never closed those doors.

I contemplated suicide. From a little girl to an adult with two children, I didn't truly understand what was happening to me. No one knew or understood what was happening to me—in fact, no one knew me. No one heard my silent cry, and I had to hold in my pain for so long that it became customary to bottle up my problems.

I know now that suicide is not the answer to any problem. It is a selfish spirit, and anyone who wants to commit suicide doesn't love themselves or anyone else. I now know that someone was willing to listen to me and know me. I know that Jesus Christ is my savior. He came so that we may have life and life more abundantly. He sacrificed His life so that we may have life, so how can we decide to take our life when it wasn't ours to take?

When the Holy Spirit led me to write and confirm this book, He knew that I needed deliverance. As I wrote it, He revealed everything I had buried so deep inside me and began uprooting it. I cried for days asking God to forgive me and to close all the open doors while writing this book. Some days I had to call out of work to deal with myself and what I was feeling and was going through. This book opened up everything that I buried so deep inside of me that I never dealt with or could talk about it. God knew how to bring it out of me so I could receive my deliverance and healing.

I know I wasn't responsible for the open door of molestation; even so, I cried for days and repented for every door that was opened. Even if I somehow opened them, even if some were my fault, I knew I had to close them. I had to become open to deliverance, and when I did, I started hearing the voice of the Holy Spirit more frequently in my life. I learned to pray and wait for his voice, receive the Word with open arms, and rest assured that prayer has power.

I wrote this book not because I wanted people to pity me or strangers to sympathize with me. I wrote it to show people the impact of spiritual open doors and what they can do to you, your children, and future generations. Once again, I was led by the Holy Spirit to write it and, most importantly, be obedient to His leading and guidance. We humans tend not to understand how our actions affect other people and the consequences that come from them. When I say other people, this includes your children as well.

This book was not to entertain but to expose the true enemy. The devil and his demons work behind the scenes when we open the door for him to use us to do his work in our lives. The devil needs a body to do his work. Many have left this earth who have been molested and had no one whom they could talk to, that dark secret place that gripped them with fear, that silent cry that no one could hear. They never had the chance to talk about what had happened to them and expose the enemy, which caused them to bury that deep hurt and pain inside of them, constantly replaying that moment in their minds.

Understanding the power of the written Word of God and the Power of the Precious Blood of Jesus Christ as you seek Him for deliverance so you can walk in divine healing from the inside out. I believe that you understand the importance of love and forgiveness, combined with the Word of God, which will help close the doors that were opened for the devil and his demons.

I pray that this book has opened your eyes so that you will know how the lack of knowledge can destroy us.

Hosea 4:6 "My people are destroyed for lack of knowledge: because thou hast rejected knowledge, I will also reject thee, that thou shalt be no priest to me: seeing thou hast forgotten the law of thy God, I will also forget thy children." (KJV)

I have shared my personal experiences and how my Lord and Savior, Jesus Christ, delivered and healed me from my past hurts and wounds! When we receive Jesus Christ as our Lord and Savior and renew our minds with the Word of God, it is more powerful than the kingdom of darkness, which is Satan and his demons. Jesus came to set the captives free. I can say that writing this book has blessed me, and I am not ashamed to talk.

I have been silent about it for many years because I did not say anything. Now, I can talk about it and confidently say I am free.

John 3:8 "He that committeth sin is of the devil; for the devil sinneth from the beginning. For this purpose the Son of God was manifested, that he might destroy the works of the devil." (KJV)

You have read about different strongholds that operate in many people's lives, and we don't even know about them due to our lack of knowledge of the Word of God.

Hosea 4:6 "My people are destroyed for lack of knowledge…" (KJV)

Corinthians 4:4 "In whom the god of this world hath blinded the minds of them which believe not, lest the light of the glorious gospel of Christ, who is the image of God, should shine unto them." (KJV)

Many of us have been deceived by the deception of the devil and his demons when we mind the things of our flesh and not by the leading of the Precious Holy Spirit. Many of us have become stuck in the areas of our lives because of the entrapments that the enemy and his demons have set up, and we don't know how to move forward. Mark 11:23 says how we can speak to our mountain to be removed from our life and not doubt in our hearts but believe we can have what we say.

Mark 11:23 "For verily I say unto you, That whosoever shall say unto this mountain, Be thou removed, and be thou cast into the sea; and shall not doubt in his heart, but shall believe that those things which he saith shall come to pass; he shall have whatsoever he saith." (KJV)

The power of our spoken words will create and frame our life. Our words can be a blessing or a curse, for we are the prophets over our own lives, for what we say and confess continually will come to pass. The Word of God can fight its own fight, especially against the kingdom of darkness. Remember when Jesus was led into the wilderness to be tempted by the devil after fasting for 40 days and 40 nights? Jesus told Him three (3) times, "It is written," for He gave the devil the written word, and the devil fled. Jesus has given us the authority to use His name and the power to tread on serpents and scorpions and over the power of the enemy, and nothing should by any means hurt us.

Luke 10:19 "Behold, I give unto you power to tread on serpents and scorpions, and over all the power of the enemy: and nothing shall by any means hurt you." (KJV)

The devil and his demons have deceived many people to reject the true and living God, for we have to seek out our own salvation with fear and trembling. How does deception deceive many? Satan has deceived many by serving false gods, false religion, and reading false doctrines, for you will see that there is only one God and there should be no other gods before Him. God said He will bless those who bless us but curse those who curse us.

Genesis 12:3: "And I will bless them that bless thee, and curse him that curseth thee:.." (KJV)

John 10:10: "The thief cometh not, but for to steal, and to kill, and to destroy: I am come that they might have life, and that they might have it more abundantly." (KJV)

I pray that your eyes of your understanding have been enlightened and that you let the Precious Holy Spirit minister to your spirit man. I pray that this book was a blessing to you as I have revealed things in this book that, once again, I am not ashamed of, and I was not to blame for what took place in my life when I was being molested, and neither are you to blame. It is not your fault.

Let us renew our minds in the Word of God and let the Word of God fight for us. Love and forgiveness are vital because we will be judged on how we treat people, not how they treat us. Every sin I have committed against God that once represented the kingdom of darkness, I have been forgiven, washed, and cleansed by the Precious Blood of my Lord and Savior, Jesus Christ, and if He did it for me, He would do it for you.

Chapter 9

How to Close Open Doors: Prayer Points

Even though I technically concluded, I didn't just want to leave you with my story and nothing else. I want to help you in the same way God has helped me. I want to show you how to close open doors.

Sin opens the door to the devil and his demons, which means our evil actions open the wrong doors. A righteous lifestyle, however, does the opposite; it closes evil doors and opens good ones in our lives. As you've learned, these things can be generationally passed down through your family bloodline, meaning you are not the only one affected by what you do.

One of the most important things we must do is first give our lives to Jesus Christ and renew our minds in the Word of God. When we stay in the Word, we renew our minds and can continue establishing a relationship with the Lord. His Word works. We must keep speaking and confessing it until we see the results.

I am now happily married to a wonderful man who loves me and is patient with me. It wasn't always this good; in the early parts of our marriage, we were headed to divorce court until the Holy Spirit came to me and asked if I would trust Him to fix my marriage, to which I replied yes, and He healed our marriage. Why am I saying this?

The door of divorce was open in my life, along with other evil things. Trusting in God is the second step in closing doors in your life after receiving Jesus Christ as your Lord and Savior and renewing your mind with the Word of God.

Everything in these following sections will be obsolete if you don't make Jesus Christ your Lord and Savior. If you are genuinely willing to take the next step to close the open doors in your life, then pray this simple prayer to be born again.

Romans 10:9-10 "That if I, shalt confess with my mouth the Lord Jesus and shalt believe in my heart that God raised Him, Jesus, from the dead, I shalt be saved. For with my heart, I believeth unto righteousness; and with my mouth confession is made unto salvation."

Father God, I thank you for your son, Jesus, who was born of the virgin Mary, and I believe he died on the cross of Calvary for our sins. I know I'm free from the curse of this world, and I fully accept what you have done for me on the cross. Being with you gives me full access to the kingdom and its resources, and I want to serve you now and for the rest of my life. I no longer rely on myself, but on you, so I thank you, Father, in Jesus' name. Amen.

First of all, welcome! With every new believer that gets saved, the hosts of heaven rejoice because you are now destined for Heaven.

However, don't think that all the benefits you enjoy are just in another realm; there are also benefits on Earth.

This next section will contain prayer points related to experiences in my life, along with some insight to explain them further. I pray these prayer points will deliver, heal, and restore you and your life. Now, you can enjoy the benefits of being a believer!

Molestation

The start of this story, unfortunately, began with me being molested. That spiral of open doors is not limited to me; sadly, it can happen to anyone. However, it is not inevitable because there are ways to spot signs in the physical and fight the problem in the spiritual. I mentioned open doors previously but wanted to discuss them here thoroughly.

The two men and the woman who molested me were operating by a spirit of lust. Something took place in each one of their lives that opened the door for them to want to have sex with a little girl. I'm not sure if someone molested them or if it was a familiar spirit in operation that was passed down from their generation because the curse was never destroyed off that bloodline. A spirit of lust is a demonic influence that one of its groupings is fornication. They had a void in their life that each one thought by fornicating with a little girl would fill, but not so.

The only way to fill any emptiness or void is to receive Jesus Christ as their Lord and Savior. When a spirit of lust is in operation, it burrows its way into people's minds, whispering to them to do evil things. The spirit of lust is only as powerful as we let it be, and it doesn't barge in; it is welcomed in.

No one in my family was aware that the man who stayed at our grandparents' house had a spirit of lust. All of us are humans and we are in the flesh, but our true person is our spirit man. When we open a door to invite someone into our home, we have given them permission to enter. This is the same way when we fornicate, commit adultery, etc., we open the doors for the devil and his demons to come in. The spirit of lust in the first man brought about the spirit of molestation in my life, which opened the door that contracted other lust spirits to me.

Spirits are not limited by space or body, so while human flesh performed the act, the spirit worked as the brain of the operation. That is why we need to understand what Paul was talking about when he said in the book of Ephesians that we don't wrestle against flesh and blood but against wicked spiritual forces.

Ephesians 6:12 "For we wrestle not against flesh and blood, but against principalities, against powers, against the rulers of the darkness of this world, against spiritual wickedness in high places." (KJV)

This is not to take the accountability away from man but to say that if we want a problem honestly solved, we need to fight the source, not the symptom. Demonic spiritual forces reveal themselves as institutional evils—genocide, terror, tyranny, and oppression.

That oppressive force was what coerced me to stay silent and being so young physically and in the Word of God, I had no natural way to counteract the problem.

In addition, the spirit of lust, which is a spirit of fornication manifested, opened the door in other ways. I am aware that both my physical parents committed adultery, which is one of the ways for lust to enter. This, coupled with the doors opened by my molesters, paved the way for me to have a promiscuous lifestyle. Doors of demonic influence can open more doors to other spirits. When someone who has sex with you can transfer other spirits from those, they slept with before you.

These same spirits can produce other things in people's lives that may not be related to one another. For example, I suffered from a strong feeling of loneliness due to the isolation. I was not invited to any of their cookouts or holiday gatherings, and some of my family members didn't want me to even engage with some of our mutual friends. I felt separated not only from my family but even from other believers, as I was judged for my past.

You already know that I was essentially chased out of the church as a result of the pastor, who had a spirit of lust, which caused his wife to have issues with me. A spirit is attracted to a familiar spirit. Meaning that a spirit of lust recognizes that same spirit in another person.

I had to walk alone, God. I had to stay close to God because He promised that He would never leave or forsake me, regardless of my past. He loves me unconditionally and forgives me for everything I have done. Loneliness, along with other things, can make it so easy for us to open the door to wrong influences or people in general who were not sent into our lives by God. Sometimes, we can let in the worst people in our lives because we want companionship.

We must learn to rely on God, regardless of what others say. I won't lie; sometimes, the words will get to you—they have gotten to me before—but learning to trust in God is a constant process.

Before we get into the prayer points, I want to speak to you as someone who was a scared child, now a caring mother and grandmother, and as someone who wishes for no other person to get hurt like that again.

We should not be so quick to let our children go with someone or spend the night at someone's house unless we are sure they are in good care. It might be a family member, like in my case, someone visiting family friends. While trusting your discernment and experiences can be effective, don't rely on that alone, and don't forget that for everything, God is willing to help. In the book of James 1:5- 7, He said that we can come to him if we lack wisdom.

James 1:5-7 *"If any of you lack wisdom, let him ask of God, that giveth to all men liberally, and upbraideth not; and it shall be given him. But let him ask in faith, nothing wavering. For he that wavereth is like a wave of the sea driven with the wind and tossed. For let not that man think that he shall receive any thing of the Lord. A double-minded man is unstable in all his ways." (KJV)*

Be on watch for signs! We as parents must establish a good and solid relationship with our children regardless of how young they are. I was not focused in elementary school because my mind was on what was happening to me. I would notice how other children were free and not daydreaming like I was doing. I wanted so much to have had a normal childhood, but all that changed because of what was happening in my life. Pay close attention to your child(ren), especially if their learning or behavior has changed and they are no longer focused.

Here are some of the things that the enemy prey on or target by molesting children:

1. They are looking for a mother, father, or both parents who want to go out and spend time alone. For example, I can babysit for you when you want to go out or enjoy some time to yourself. (This can be a male or female.)
2. A mother, father, or both parents are not involved in the lives of their child(ren), just thinking about themselves.
3. No father in the house or maybe not the mother in the house.
4. There is no relationship between the parents and the child(ren), so they can easily keep a secret and not talk to their parents about anything.
5. Parent(s) who are not involved in any relationship with their child(ren) who work all the time and let them raise themselves.
6. Be careful who you let enter your home or stay with you.
7. Don't let your children sit on someone's lap, especially in the middle.
8. Be very cautious about letting your child(ren) go to someone's house for sleepovers.

Protect your children because they can't protect themselves. Again, I want to stress that you should be mindful of who your children hang around with. You must know with surety that they are around godly people with a strong spirit of discernment and don't just let anyone in your household.

Also, it doesn't matter if you're letting your son spend the night with a male friend of theirs or your daughter spend the night with a female friend of theirs; that perverse spirit does not care for gender. It will be used by whoever opens the door to it.

Give yourself to the Lord and sharpen your prayer life. Pray for yourself, your children, and every area of your life. Don't make room for the devil; only make room for Christ Jesus.

Matthew 9:1-2 shows how sin in a person's life can cause sicknesses and diseases. When a man was paralyzed because of the sins he committed, doors were opened in his life. It took the mighty power of Jesus to close those doors by forgiving him of his sins. I bring up this story because we have that mighty power in us now; we have scriptures to call God to the scene. So, I will help you sharpen your prayer life with these scriptures and prayer points so you, too, can conquer the works of the enemy:

Matthew 9:1-2 "And he entered into a ship, and passed over, and came into his own city. And, behold, they brought to him a man sick of the palsy, lying on a bed: and Jesus seeing their faith said unto

the sick of the palsy; Son, be of good cheer; thy sins be forgiven thee." (KJV)

1 Peter 5:8 "Most importantly, be disciplined and stay on guard. Your enemy the devil is prowling around outside like a roaring lion, just waiting and hoping for the chance to devour someone." (The Voice)

Prayer point: Father God, I ask you to forgive me of all my sins. You said that if I confess my sins, you are faithful and just to forgive me of all my sins and cleanse me of all unrighteousness. I thank you for blessing me with a spirit of discernment to see and prevent the enemy's works. Even though he is prowling, he will not come near me or my household because I close all doors that I have given the devil and his demons permission to come in, and I lock and seal them doors by the Precious Blood of Jesus Christ. Amen.

Psalm 32:8-9 "I hear the Lord saying, "I will stay close to you, instructing and guiding you along the pathway for your life. I will advise you along the way and lead you forth with my eyes as your guide. So don't make it difficult; don't be stubborn when I take you where you've not been before. Don't make me tug you and pull you along. Just come with me!" (TPT)

Prayer Point: Father God, I thank you for your guidance. I pray that I will not make it hard for you to guide me; instead, I will obey your leadership and guidance everywhere and every step I take. I pray that I am following your truth and not relying on myself for protection. In Jesus' name. Amen.

Luke 10:19 "Now you understand that I have imparted to you my authority to trample over his kingdom. You will trample upon every demon before you and overcome every power Satan possesses. Absolutely nothing will harm you as you walk in this authority." (TPT)

Prayer Point: I thank Father God for giving me the authority to trample over the kingdom of darkness. I pray, Father, for the wisdom and boldness to put a halt to Satan's plans over my life, my family's life, and the lives of those around me. I shut every door that needs to be closed for your will to be done in my life, in Jesus' name, Amen.

Hosea 4:6 "My people are destroyed for lack of knowledge: because thou hast rejected knowledge, I will also reject thee, that thou shalt be no priest to me: seeing thou hast forgotten the law of thy God, I will also forget thy children." (KJV)

Prayer Point: Thank you, Father God, for giving me the knowledge and understanding of the enemy's works. I pray, Father God, that I accept your knowledge; instead, I use what I know to close the doors that the devil has opened in my life. Help me, Father God, to not open any more doors for the enemy. Instead, the only important door I desire to open is when you knock on the door of my heart, which is godly. I thank you, Father, in Jesus' name, Amen.

Romans 12:1-2 "Beloved friends, what should be our proper response to God's marvelous mercies? To surrender yourselves to God to be his sacred, living sacrifices. And live in holiness, experiencing all that delights his heart. For this becomes your genuine expression of worship. Stop imitating the ideals and opinions of the culture around you, but be inwardly transformed by the Holy Spirit through a total reformation of how you think. This will empower you to discern God's will as you live a beautiful life, satisfying and perfect in his eyes." (TPT)

Prayer Point: Father God, I dedicate my life to you and offer myself as a living sacrifice, meaning that I forsake the lusts of my flesh and follow your wondrous ways for my life. I thank you, Father, for giving me a beautiful life, and I pray I will not turn from you by following my flesh. I thank you, Father, in Jesus' name. Amen.

Before this next prayer point, I want to say something. I understand this is a complicated request, and I do not make it in ignorance, nor do I do it with a lack of empathy. Still, I ask that if anyone has been molested, raped, abused physically, mentally, and verbally, please forgive those who have harmed you. Forgiveness is not for the other person; it is for you.

This was probably the hardest thing I had to do; it took me years to find the place to do it, but God can help even through the harshest of experiences. When He said He is a comforter and a guide, those titles aren't for show; He means it.

Mark 11:25-26 "And whenever you stand praying, if you find that you carry something in your heart against another person, release him and forgive him so that your Father in heaven will also release you and forgive you of your faults. But if you will not release forgiveness, don't expect your Father in heaven to release you from your misdeeds." (TPT)

Prayer Point: Father God, give me the spirit of forgiveness and help me keep it open perpetually in my life. I do not want to walk in unforgiveness anymore; instead, I want to walk in perpetual forgiveness, as you have with the entire human race. I open the door to forgiveness and close the door to unforgiveness, commanding anything that unforgiveness has wrought in my life to be removed. I speak wholeness to my body, in Jesus' name, Amen.

Now, if there is someone who is reading this book and you have been the one used by the devil to abuse innocent children sexually, verbally, and physically, please cry out to God for Him to forgive you because He Loves you so very much that He gave His only Begotten Son to die on the Cross (John 3:16) for you. Hurting people hurts other people.

Mark 7:20-23: "He added, "Words and deeds pollute a person, not food. Evil originates from inside a person. Coming out of a human heart are evil schemes," sexual immorality, theft, murder, adultery, greed, wickedness, treachery, debauchery, jealousy, slander, arrogance, and recklessness. All these corrupt things emerge from within and constantly defile a person." (TPT)

Galatians 5:19-21: "The behavior of the self-life is obvious: Sexual immorality, lustful thoughts, pornography, chasing after things instead of God, manipulating others, hatred of those who get in your way, senseless arguments, resentment when others are favored, temper tantrums, angry quarrels, only thinking of yourself, being in love with your own opinions, being envious of the blessings of others, murder, uncontrolled addictions, wild parties, and all other similar behavior. Haven't I already warned you that those who use their" freedom" for these things will not inherit the kingdom realm of God!" (TPT)

God will forgive you no matter what, but you must commit to changing your life, following Him, and, most importantly, forgiving yourself.

I want to make this declaration myself. If any of the people who molested me are still living, I write it now in this book that I forgive you and find no fault in you. I truly pray that you learn to receive the love of God and accept Him into your life. I also pray that you no longer make way for the devil and his demons in your life. God loves you and will forgive you if you go to Him.

John 3:16 "For here is the way God loved the world-he gave his only, unique Son as a gift. So now everyone who believes in him will never perish but experience everlasting life." (TPT)

The last thing I want to say in this section is that I don't blame anyone for what has occurred in my life since I have grown up spiritually in the Word of God; I find no fault in them. If you used drugs, alcohol, and anything else to help block out what you were going through, it is not the answer. Also, suicide is not the answer. When our thoughts are entertaining or contemplating suicide, it is from the devil because God has blessed us with life, and who are we to end the life He has blessed us with? A person who does that has a selfish spirit, and not only that, but they don't love themselves, and they don't love anyone else. Jesus Christ has been my counselor and delivered me from my past hurts and pains, and He is no respecter of person; he will heal and deliver you.

When He led me to write this book, He knew it would uproot everything deeply buried inside me so He could set me free. If He did it for me, He will do it for you.

Playing House

Another open door that needs to be addressed is the spirit of lust which is a demonic influence that one of its groupings is homosexuality. We have already established that actions can open the doors for spirits, and those same spirits can open the doors for other spirits. So, homosexuality itself is a result of a spirit of lust along with its other groupings, adultery, fornication, etc.

As stated in prior chapters, this young girl from my neighborhood wanted to play "House," which involved two women kissing and fondling one another. Despite not being a teenager, she was open to us engaging in adult activities. Doors produce after their kind, meaning that when a door is opened in one person's life, it wishes to open itself in someone else's.

God created man and woman for each other, as stated in the beginning chapters of Genesis.

Genesis 2:21-25 *"So the Eternal God put him into a deep sleep, removed a rib from his side, and closed the flesh around the opening. He formed a woman from the rib taken out of the man and presented her to him. Adam: At last, a suitable companion, a perfect partner. Bone from my bones. Flesh from my flesh. I will call this one "woman" as an eternal reminder that she was taken out of man. Now this is the reason a man leaves his father and his mother and is united with his*

wife, and the two become one flesh. In those days the man and his wife were both naked and were not ashamed."

1 Corinthians 15:33 "Do not be so deceived and misled! Evil companionships (communion, associations) corrupt and deprave good manners and morals and character."

As parents, grandparents, and guardians, we must be mindful of where our children stay, not just infants, toddlers, and kids but also teenagers. As long as they are under our roofs and even beyond, we must be on the lookout for things trying to corrupt them. Being a parent is more than just birthing children; it is looking out for them, teaching them, and covering the weak points they cannot see. That means who they associate themselves with, whose house they spend the night at, who they date, and even the friends of the people they hang with.

A homosexual is a spirit of lust that can be borne from abuse and evil exposure (hence why some people who are raped or molested become homosexuals in the future) and can be born from a lack of love. We should learn the difference between loving the person and not tolerating the spirit. A person who is living a homosexual lifestyle is still God's child, and we should treat them as such, but we should not tolerate that spirit that is in operation in their life. I had to stand against that spirit of lust because of the doors that were opened in my life. I had to demand that curse spirit of lust of homosexuality be uprooted and destroyed out of my life and the life of my children, grandchildren and generations to come.

See, when we think wrong, we do wrong, and our thinking

becomes a mindset that has not been renewed by the Word of God. A person with a perverted mindset believes that the lifestyle of two men or two women sleeping together is normal when it is not. Although it happened to me when I was a little girl and when I played house with another female, it was wrong and perverted.

God's Word says that our thoughts are not His thoughts, and our ways are not His ways (Isaiah 55:8-9). God created a man and a woman, and He blessed their union, for that is the correct sexual behavior.

Isaiah 55:8-9 "Eternal One: My intentions are not always yours, and I do not go about things as you do. My thoughts and My ways are above and beyond you, just as heaven is far from your reach here on earth." (The Voice)

Once again, we do things out of a lack of knowledge, not knowing how it can and will affect our lives. Read the story of Sodom and Gomorrah. Sodom and Gomorrah's sin was sexual immorality, which included homosexuality. Abraham's nephew Lot lived there in the City of Sodom until God sent two (2) men who were His angels to destroy the city. The men in the city begged Lot to send them out so they could be with them, for they didn't know the men were angels sent by God. The sent angels by God told Lot to hurry up and take his family and leave and not look back because they were sent to destroy that city which the Lord rained upon Sodom and Gomorrah brimstone and fire from the Lord out of heaven. (Read the story about

Sodom and Gomorrah Genesis 19:1-29)

2 Peter 2:6 "And don't forget that he reduced to ashes the cities of Sodom and Gomorrah, condemning them to ruin and destruction. God appointed them to be examples as to what is coming to the ungodly."

Deuteronomy 22:5 "A woman must not wear men's clothing, and men must not put on women's garments. The Eternal your God is horrified when anyone does this."

Isaiah 55:8-9 "For my thoughts are not your thoughts, neither are your ways my ways, saith the Lord For as the heavens are higher than the earth, so are my ways higher than your ways, and my thoughts than your thoughts."

Prayer Point: Father God, I first want to repent by trying to judge your ways according to my understanding. I pray that I can see things the way you see them and judge thoughts as you would. In Jesus' name, Amen.

Leviticus 18:22 "Thou shalt not lie with mankind, as with womankind, it is abomination."

Prayer Point: Father God, I pray that I am not engaging in behaviors that are not an abomination to you. I pray that you are releasing me from any hold of homosexuality in my life. I am freed from this spirit, close the door to it in my generation, and cleanse my entire Bloodline with the Precious Blood of Jesus Christ. I thank you, Father, in Jesus' name, Amen.

Abortion

I have already talked about some of the doors that were swung open because of the molestation that had happened to me. However, there is one that I wanted to give its section since it's too familiar today.

When I was 13, I had my first abortion because I was sexually active. Again, I have already stated that doors take after their kind, and with so many sexual partners, abortion seemed to be the next step.

Taking the life of an unborn child is wrong, no matter how you spin it or package it. When I took the life of my first child, I became numb to abortion and had so many afterward. I had to ask the Lord to forgive me because the devil was using me to enact such an evil deed. For the devil come to steal, kill, and destroy, but Jesus came that we might have life and that we might have life more abundantly.

Children are a gift from God to us so we can experience the wonders of parenthood ourselves. When we destroy our children, we ruin our future. No matter how much success we have in life, if we don't have a successor, a child, or children to carry it on, we have destroyed more than we have created.

Although my mother has been through a lot, she could have aborted me and my brothers, but she didn't; instead, she kept us. Yes, I've made many mistakes, but my life is the Lord's, and He's helped me and delivered me from all my past abuse, hurts, and pain.

Many use abortions as a form of contraception. When a woman aborts a life, they destroy the destiny, plan, and purpose that God had given them before they were in their mother's womb. God had a relationship with us before we were formed. Before we took our first breath, He already had chosen us.

God already had a relationship with each one of us before we were in our mother's womb; however, if the mother never read the Word of God to her child(ren) and even when they were born, it divided the relationship that they had with their real Heavenly Father. Even if you have to give your child up for adoption, you didn't abort it.

Here are a few scriptures and prayer points concerning this subject:

Jeremiah 1:5 "Eternal One: Before I even formed you in your mother's womb, I knew all about you. Before you drew your first breath, I had already chosen you..." (The Voice)

1 John 1:9 "But if we freely admit our sins when his light uncovers them, he will be faithful to forgive us every time. God is just to forgive us our sins because of Christ, and he will continue to cleanse us from all unrighteousness."

Prayer Point: Father God, I ask for forgiveness for aborting your child. I know that children are your gift, and I repent for cutting short a life made to serve you. I thank you for your forgiveness, in Jesus' name. Amen.

Jeremiah 29:11-14 "For I know the plans I have for you," says the Eternal, "plans for peace, not evil, to give you a future and hope—never forget that. At that time, you will call out for Me, and I will hear.

You will pray, and I will listen. You will look for Me intently, and you will find Me. Yes, I will be found by you," says the Eternal,..."

Prayer Point: Father God, I know you have a plan for me, a plan of prosperity and not disaster. I pray that I and my children will walk according to your plan. I know that plan doesn't involve me aborting children but teaching and nurturing them how to live a godly life. I thank you, Father, that I will walk according to your plan. In Jesus' name. Amen.

Here are some other scriptures about God having a plan for us and our children (no prayer points attached):

Ephesians 1:11 *"Through our union with Christ we too have been claimed by God as his own inheritance. Before we were even born, he gave us our destiny; that we would fulfill the plan of God who always accomplishes every purpose and plan in his heart."*

Ephesians 2:10 *"We have become his poetry, a re-created people that will fulfill the destiny he has given each of us, for we are joined to Jesus, the Anointed One. Even before we were born, God planned in advance our destiny and the good works we would do to fulfill it!"*

Ezekiel 37:5-6 *"Eternal One: Actually, I do. Prophesy to these bones. Tell them to listen to what the Eternal Lord says to them: "Dry bones, I will breathe breath into you, and you will come alive. I will attach muscles and tendons to you, cause flesh to grow over them, and cover you with skin. I will breathe breath into you, and you will come* *alive. After this happens, you will know that I am the Eternal." "God is not only the Creator of life, but He is also the Restorer of life."*

Psalm 139:13-16 "I will offer You my grateful heart, for I am Your unique creation, filled with wonder and awe. You have approached even the smallest details with excellence; Your works are wonderful; I carry this knowledge deep within my soul. You see all things; nothing about me was hidden from You As I took shape in secret, carefully crafted in the heart of the earth before I was born from its womb. You see all things; You saw me growing, changing in my mother's womb; Every detail of my life was already written in Your book; You established the length of my life before I ever tasted the sweetness of it."

Jeremiah 1:5 "Eternal One: Before I even formed you in your mother's womb, I knew all about you. Before you drew your first breath, I had already chosen you to be My prophet to speak My word to the nations."

I want to tell you a short story to end this section. My oldest grandson, who was nine then, went to bed one night and had a visitation from Jesus. He toured my grandson through different parts of Heaven, seeing other children playing and having fun. The children? Some of those who were aborted and those who were taken before their time.

Your spirit man is the real you. The spirit is called a man's heart because it is the core or center of his being and the life of the body.

When the spirit leaves the body, the body dies, but your spirit man lives forever. When you give your life to Jesus Christ, you will see your aborted child(ren) again.

Prayer Point: Father God, I know you have a plan for me, a plan of prosperity and not disaster. I pray that my child(ren) and I will walk according to your plan. I know that plan doesn't involve me aborting my child(ren) but teaching and nurturing them how to live a godly life. I thank you, Father, that I will walk according to your plan. In the name Lord Jesus Christ." Amen.

Sexual Immorality Which Can Lead to Sexual Transmitted Diseases (STDs)

While looking for love in all the wrong places, I brought up a series of problems to myself. In the last section, I'm sure you've noticed that everything I have encountered in my life was caused by one open door spiraling out of control. The longer I stayed in that maze, the thorn of the bushes got me at every turn.

When the spirit of lust enters, many things follow that we expect and things that we don't understand. Many Christians think that everything is a spirit, but not quite. Spirits have different forms of manifestation or groupings, so a spirit of lust can manifest as a physical infirmity, a mental issue, or even a hard-to-break habit. We must be aware of every aspect of these problems and address them accordingly.

As for (STDs) it is another way of interacting with someone in adultery and fornication that can bring about a ruin to our bodies. When we are fornicating and committing adultery, whomever that person slept with the same spirits is transferred to you, for we become one with that person.

This is another open door for the enemy and his demon(s) to enter when we commit fornication and adultery. Our body is the temple of the Holy Spirit, so we must not defile it because when we sleep with another person, we become one with that person. Please see the scripture listed below, Matthew 19:4-6, which explains how God created us to be sexually active when we are married, not being single or married, having sex outside of marriage.

Matthew 19:4-6 "Haven't you read the Scriptures about creation?" Jesus replied. "The Creator made us male and female from the very beginning, and 'For this reason a man will leave his father and mother and live with his wife. And the two will become one flesh.' From then on, they are no longer two, but united as one. So what God unites let no one divide!" (TPT)

No one bears a unique appearance when they have STDs unless they are in the final stages. Some STDs are incurable by human standards. Nothing is impossible for God; however, we shouldn't tempt God by allowing these spirits in our lives by committing sexual immorality.

We should not be so quick to join ourselves with someone sexually because when we become one with that person, we connect to them. We need to educate on STDs because they are transferred from one person to another just like a spirit of lust can be transferred.

1 John 4:1 "My loved ones, I warn you: do not trust every spirit. Instead, examine them carefully to determine if they come from God..." (The Voice)

1 Corinthians 6:15-20 "Don't you know that your bodies belong to Christ as his body parts? Should one presume to take the members of Christ's body and make them into members of a harlot? Absolutely not! Aren't you aware of the fact that when anyone sleeps with a

prostitute he becomes a part of her, and she becomes a part of him? For it has been declared: But the one who joins himself to the Lord is mingled into one spirit with him. This is why you must keep running away from sexual immorality. For every other sin a person commits is external to the body, but immorality involves sinning against your own body. Have you forgotten that your body is now the sacred temple of the Spirit of Holiness, who lives in you? You don't belong to yourself any longer, for the gift of God, the Holy Spirit, lives inside your sanctuary. You were God's expensive purchase, paid for with tears of blood, so by all means, then, use your body to bring glory to God!" (TPT)

Prayer Point: Father God, thank you for making me a temple for your glory. I first repent for taking my body lightly and letting it be used for evil. I cast out the spirit of lust that I have allowed in my life, and I close the door and lock and seal it with the Precious Blood of Jesus Christ. Thanks for restoring my soul and leading me in the path of righteousness for His name sake, and I receive your divine healing in Jesus' name." Amen.

Everyone Behind the Pulpit Is Not Called by God.

Seek God for everyday guidance and direction in your life, including which church He will have you attend.

I love being a believer; it is the best thing that ever happened to me. Understanding and fixing the problems in my life gave me so much release and freedom. However, I also know that every person who claims to be of God may not be of God.

When the pastor was asked to pray for my condo, he had another motive. A True man of God should not open themselves to such an evil spirit of lust. I don't know if he was called, but one thing is for sure: God did not support what he did to me.

God has strict criteria that his leaders must follow. The word leader is often used, yet it is powerful. A leader is a role model, a guide, a director, and a peacemaker. God's laws ensure that his leaders are people of righteousness.

I am thankful that the Holy Spirit told me that some churches were not of him and that not everyone behind a pulpit is called.
The Lord gave me three (3) reasons why we need to seek Him for which church we should attend. (1). Everyone behind the pulpit is not sent by God. (2). People are leaving out the same way they came in. (3). They must be sent by Him.

The influences you listen to are in conjunction with the spirits you entertain. If you consume media that contains sex, violence, foul and/or corrupt language, etc. or are around people who entertain those things, that same spirit will have the opportunity to transfer to you. When we give place to these kinds of things, we can open the door for the devil and his demons to enter. You will give the devil the chance to enter your life and your home. In my case, it may not be you but your children or someone else who suffers.

Conversely, if you entertain godly media, such as Bible teaching, praise and worship, Christian television, and reading the Bible, and/or surround yourself with people who do those things, you will entertain God and godly spirits.

We must seek God for direction, guidance, and wisdom, especially which church He would have us attend. Everyone behind that pulpit is not sent by God.

Talking about this is near and dear to me, not simply because of the pastor who tried to sleep with me but also because of a situation that happened with my mother. To make it short, my mother went to see a pastor for advice and guidance, only to find out that this man was a voodoo doctor. He did strange things to my mother, opening the door for other spirits to enter her life. Her mood and demeanor changed, and that was one of the reasons why she pulled a knife on me so many years ago.

I grew up in a lot of areas, especially when it came to my mother. I didn't know she'd been through a lot and didn't know how to love. It is hard to love someone else if we don't love ourselves.

I thank God my mother is freed from such things, and our relationship has only improved. I have forgiven her for everything that was done and said to me. We call each other, laugh, and talk, and I make sure whatever my mother needs is taken care of because I find no fault in her and don't hold anything against her because it wasn't her doing. When we realize that when we open doors that look so innocence, it can come with a cost. If my mother knew that the Pastor that was behind that pulpit was a voodoo doctor, she would have left and not entertained it.

My mother did the best she could for my brothers and me. Regardless of the choices and decisions that were made in her life, I love her so very much; she is my mother.

Yes, we didn't always have food to eat all the time, or the gas was turned off, so there was no hot water to take a bath or stove to cook on, and many times the rent was past due, but I thank God for our grandmother, my mother's mom, who would step in and help us when she could.

Healing like this takes time, but we must find it in our hearts to start the process. We have to put the work in. It also takes a mindset shift. I have seen my mother come through so much, and she never aborted me or gave me up for adoption; she didn't. Thinking like this, my heart is filled with more and more compassion for her and everyone else in my life. The enemy tried to destroy the relationship between my mother and me; the doors were opened that had caused division and separation among us. Still, since our mother-and-daughter relationship has been restored, I am so grateful.

But I digress; the purpose of this part is to remind us that we should not simply go to a church just because it is nearby or because the pastor is well-known or liked. We can't just attend a church because it was a family church or the religion you were raised by or introduced to; I can only suggest that you seek the true and living God for direction, and He is our Lord and Savior, Jesus Christ the only one that gave His Life so that we may have an abundant Life and live. We can't come to the Father (God) unless we come through His Son, our Lord, and Savior Jesus Christ. I will tell this last story before we get to the prayer points.

Once again, this is a true story. God gave me the vision to get personalized balloons made with healing scriptures and one that said, "Jesus is Lord." They were to be delivered to people in the hospital. I would explain to them why they should confess Jesus is Lord and also confess healing scriptures over their lives.

I received a phone call from a young lady ordering healing scripture balloons for a co-worker who was in the final stages of AIDS. They did not expect her to come home because of the doctor's report, so I prayed and fasted, got the balloons together, and took them to her. She was a young girl, and upon seeing her, it was apparent that she had lost much weight. I explained the "Jesus is Lord" and the Healing Scripture Balloons, and then I started praying for her. When I laid my hands on her and started praying, the voice of the Holy Spirit spoke through me, and when I touched her, the Power of God flowed from me to her with electricity flowing through my whole body into hers.

I was in training by the Holy Spirit and didn't know much about Divine Healing. The following week, I received a phone call from the young lady who ordered the balloons for her co-worker. She was so happy because the young lady who was in the hospital received her healing and was made whole. The Holy Spirit spoke to me and asked me to ask the lady to have her give me a call because He had a Word for her. The young lady who was healed from AIDS called me, and the Holy Spirit told me to tell her that she needed to be in a word-teaching church so she could keep her healing, but the young lady said that she couldn't because she went to a family church and her family would disapprove of it. Much later, I received a phone call that she had died.

That is why it is so vital that we seek God for which church to attend and be obedient. The keys to our destiny and the maintenance of our lives cannot be found anywhere; they are found where God ordained us.

Ephesians 4:11-13 "And he has appointed some with grace to be apostles, and some with grace to be prophets, and some with grace to be evangelists, and some with grace to be pastors, and some with grace to be teachers. And their calling is to nurture and prepare all the holy believers to do their own works of ministry, and as they do this they will enlarge and build up the body of Christ. These grace ministries will function until we all attain oneness into the faith, until we all experience the fullness of what it means to know the Son of

God, and finally we become one into a perfect man with the full dimensions of spiritual maturity and fully developed into the abundance of Christ." (TPT)

Prayer Point: Father God, you have created the fivefold ministry to edify and perfect your church. I ask for guidance and knowledge to know who is of you and to lead me in the way of righteousness in Jesus' name. I pray that I will also be able to discern those who are not of you, so I do not open any more evil doors in my life. Thank you for your edification through the people you have ordained and sent; I thank you again, in Jesus' name. Amen.

John 14:26 "But when the Father sends the Spirit of Holiness, the One like me who sets you free, he will teach you all things in my name. And he will inspire you to remember every word that I've told you."
(TPT)

Prayer Point: Father God, thank you for the Precious Holy Spirit that you sent to us, your children. I pray that my immaturity will end so that I will be your mature child who will be moved by the impulses of the Holy Spirit and will not act against it in any shape or form. I repent if I have, and I pray that my life is in your perfect will in the name of Jesus. Also, I pray that I will be led by the Holy Spirit in order to connect with people, pastors, and friends who also have this Spirit of Holiness so we can work in all godliness as a body. I thank you, Father, in Jesus' name. Amen.

Jeremiah 3:15 "Then I will give you shepherds who trust and know Me, wise teachers who will impart knowledge and understanding to you." (The Voice)

Prayer Point: Father God, thank you for giving me a shepherd who has a heart after you God. I pray that you are leading me to the right one who will help me in my God-given destiny, purpose, and plan after your heart, God, that will come to pass in my life. I pray that the spirit of obedience rests upon me as I listen to them and that they will never depart from your Word. I thank you, Father God, in Jesus' name. Amen.

Romans 10:14-15 "How then shall they call on him in whom they have not believed? and how shall they believe in him of whom they have not heard? and how shall they hear without a preacher? And how shall they preach, except they be sent? as it is written, How beautiful are the feet of them that preach the gospel of peace, and bring glad tidings of good things!" (KJV)

Prayer Point: I pray, Father God, that I am being put in the path of a pastor who teaches your unadulterated word, one who is sent by you and flows by your spirit. If I am already under a person like that, I pray they continue to teach your Word so that I will walk in your perfect will and that your peace is beyond any and all of my understanding, and I thank you, Father, in Jesus' name. Amen.

Unforgiveness

Many of us have experienced deep pain from what we have endured, which may have birthed unforgiveness in us. Sometimes, we still feel the burning hatred when we think about specific people, places, or memories.

I know how unforgiveness feels. It eats at you like a parasite, draining your happiness and injecting malice. We know we should let go, and sometimes we even try to reason with ourselves why the other person is not at fault, but that doesn't always work. Unforgiveness pushed me into the arms of people who didn't have my best interest at heart; it led me down a path where I thought I was safe. Some people manifest their unforgiveness as apathy, gossip, hatred, etc.

While changing our mindset is good, we need something much more tangible to hold onto –the Word. If you're looking for ease, you are mistaken, but if we do what God's Word says, we can do it. We can do everything through Christ Jesus, who strengthens us regardless of situation or circumstances. Yes, our flesh will get in the way because it has controlled us for so long that we must put our flesh under subjection.

Once we keep speaking and believing the Word of God, it will uproot everything that represents the kingdom of darkness. However, we must accept that the Word of God will work for us, which requires our faith. The Word of God is seed, so it is up to us to plant the seed in us so it will grow and produce life. Whatever we need, salvation, deliverance, healing, prosperity, etc., is in the Word of God. Our heart consists of four (4) kinds of "soils": 1) the human Heart, 2). Shallow Heart, 3). Half/Worldly Heart, 4.) Whole/Rooted and Grounded Heart.

1 Peter 1:23: "For through the eternal and living Word of God you have been born again. And this "seed" that he planted within you can never be destroyed but will live and grow inside of you forever..." (TPT)

Unforgiveness has physical side effects due to its impact on our minds. It is a poison to our minds and our health. Dr. Don Colbert wrote a book about Deadly Emotions, which discusses incurable sicknesses and diseases that come from unforgiveness; however, you can overcome these deadly emotions by forgiving.

Forgiveness was never indeed for the other person; it was for the person who was wronged. Not forgiving someone gives them the power to affect your mind and health. It took me time to think about that myself. Unforgiveness allows people to gain control over us. Those who hurt us could be living their lives, being happy, getting married, and even giving their lives to Christ; all the while, we stand with a heart of unforgiveness, that opens the door for sicknesses and diseases.

Many times, people don't know they have offended someone unless they are told or confronted. Those people might have already asked God to forgive them and are moving on if they know they have offended you. Offense is a bait of Satan.

When we apply the Word of God to a situation alongside love and forgiveness, we close the door to the enemy and open the door to healing our physical body so we can walk in divine health. Healing manifests in our spirit, soul, and body.

In January 2013, the doctor tried to diagnose me with an incurable disease. When man says it is incurable, remember that it is their words, not what God says, so I decided to stand on the Word of God for my healing. As leaving the doctor's office, they offered me some medication, and I told them that I already had medicine that I would be taking, and that was the Word of God.

In 2016, I started feeling symptoms, and fear tried to come upon me. I started seeking Naturopathic doctors because the doctors could not help me. I found a doctor who gave me some natural instructions to follow, and I did. it caused me to lose so much weight that I went from 155lbs to 103lbs and wore a size 0. I was walking slower than a turtle and was in a lot of pain 24 hours a day, non-stop. I was walking up and down the steps, taking one step at a time, holding on to the rail, and it took me a very long time to get to where I needed to go.

One morning, I went to work, and my supervisor and Deputy Director called me into their office with many concerns because they noticed the change in my weight and how I looked. My supervisor suggested that I leave on temporary disability, and I started crying and said I was not going on no disability, so they asked me to take some leave so I could get myself together, and I did. I took almost six (6) weeks of leave and used that opportunity to stay in the Word of God morning, noon, and night every day for six weeks. The outside still looked the same, but the Word of God was working on the inside of me. When I returned to work, I was still walking very slowly; however, I kept confessing healing scriptures as I sat down and when I got up walking. I would sit down, and it took me a very long time to get out of a chair; many have offered to help me, but I would say healed people get up, and I would thank them for wanting to be a blessing to me, however; it was so hard, and I knew that I needed help so I forced myself to do the things that I usually would do.

My husband and my youngest daughter would help me at home, but I did it regardless of how long it took. I was in so much pain that I picked up the phone to call someone to pray for me, and the Holy Spirit spoke to me and said, "Don't call no one to pray for you; just keep confessing His Word – not recalling every word that He said but He wanted me to continue to trust Him even when it was feeling like I was getting worse."

One day, without realizing it, I was walking normal, going up and down the steps normally, gaining my weight back, and all the pain was gone. To God be all the Glory! I had to not focus on my current circumstances, not the pain and what I was seeing, because it is the healing Word of God that gets rid of every lying symptom and washes all sicknesses, diseases, and pain. When we speak the living Word of God over our body, it is the flow of the Word that manifests the healing. 2 Corinthians 4:18 tells us not to look at what is seen, even go by what we feel, but look at what is not seen, as Jesus is the author and finisher of our Faith.

2 Corinthians 4:18 "While we look not at the things which are seen, but at the things which are not seen: for the things which are seen are temporary; but the things which are not seen are eternal." (KJV)

My husband and I went to Florida to visit Dr. Don Colbert, and as he was examining me, he asked me a question: what was my childhood like? Did anything traumatic happen to you? That is when he explained to me how what happened to me opened the door to that disease that tried to attack my health because of deadly emotions. I had buried everything so deep inside me and never talked about it as the root cause of what the doctor tried to diagnose me with. When the Holy Spirit spoke to me and said, "I am delivering you; don't let no one keep you in bondage," that included me being delivered from my past, including all sicknesses, diseases, and pain, and healing was manifested in my body. I was made whole, spirit, soul, and body.

Believe the Word of God only, and don't stop until you see the manifestation. Even if some symptoms have left and you are feeling much better, keep speaking and standing on the Word of God until all symptoms are gone because Jesus does not do partial healings. These symptoms and afflictions will not rise the second time in your life in the name of the Lord Jesus Christ, so be it!

Forgive those who hurt you, and most importantly, forgive yourself. Work on yourself and get to the root of your issues and problems. God knew I needed deliverance, and the root of the cause was what happened in my childhood.

Listed below are some of the categories that are listed in Dr. Don Colbert's book called "Deadly Emotions":

1. **Anger and Hostility** – can cause Hypertension and Coronary Artery Disease
2. **Resentment, Bitterness, Unforgiveness, and Self-Hatred** – can cause Autoimmune Disorders, Rheumatoid Arthritis, Lupus, and Multiple Sclerosis
3. **Anxiety** – can cause Irritable Bowel Syndrome, Panic Attacks, Mitral Valve Prolapse, and Heart Palpitations
4. **Repressed Anger** – can cause Tension and Migraine Headaches, Chronic Back Pain, TMJ, and Fibromyalgia

I had to forgive those who molested me and those who hurt me, including the person who hurt my baby girl. God's Word is full of life and health if we apply it, but we must sow the seed, which is the engrafted Word of God. Why should we risk all these diseases because of someone else? I don't know about you, but risking these diseases is not worth the trouble. Even spiritually, we must understand that our Heavenly Father will not forgive us if we don't forgive others.

We must read the word and meditate on it day and night. Why? so we can embody the word, making it easier for us to forgive and understand forgiveness.

The Holy Spirit told me, "When you can write about it and talk about it, you are delivered." However, the enemy will try to keep bringing up your past, and you must cast down them imaginations once again as they come and stand on the integrity of God's Word.

***2 Corinthians 10:3-6** "For though we walk in the world, we do not fight according to this world's rules of warfare. The weapons of the war we're fighting are not of this world but are powered by God and effective at tearing down the strongholds erected against His truth. We are demolishing arguments and ideas, every high-and-mighty philosophy that pits itself against the knowledge of the one true God. We are taking prisoners of every thought, every emotion, and subduing them into obedience to the Anointed One. As soon as you choose obedience, we stand ready to punish every act of disobedience." (The Voice)*

***Mark 11:25-26** "And whenever you stand praying, if you find that you carry something in your heart against another person, release him and forgive him so that your Father in heaven will also release you and forgive you of your faults. But if you will not release forgiveness, don't expect your Father in heaven to release you from your misdeeds." (TPT)*

Prayer Point: Father God, in Jesus' name, I thank you for forgiving my sins. Even though I was against you, you have still accepted me. Lord God, give me the strength to extend that same forgiveness to those who have wronged me so you can hear my prayers and release me from my faults. I pray this in the name of the Lord Jesus Christ. Amen.

Proverbs 14:29-30 *"People with understanding control their anger; a hot temper shows great foolishness. A peaceful heart leads to a healthy body; jealousy is like cancer in the bones." (NLT)*

Prayer Point: I pray, Father God, that I am among the people who understand and can control their anger. I pray, Father God, that you are helping me control my anger so I can have a peaceful heart. I will not be jealous; I will live healthy and happily. I thank you, Father, in Jesus' name. Amen.

Romans 12:19-21 *"Dear friends, never take revenge. Leave that to the righteous anger of God. For the Scriptures say, "I will take revenge; I will pay them back," says the LORD. Instead, "If your enemies are hungry, feed them. If they are thirsty, give them something to drink. In doing this, you will heap burning coals of shame on their heads." Don't let evil conquer you but conquer evil by doing good." (NLT)*

Prayer Point: Father God, I thank you for the spirit of love that will rest upon me as I go through life. Help my heart to be eased so that I do not take revenge on those who have wronged me. I leave them up to you, Father, and I ask for your great love to rest upon me so that if I see my enemies again, I will find it in my heart to pray for them and forgive them. I thank you, Father, in Jesus' name, Amen.

Be Obedient to the Voice of the Holy Spirit

Obedience is necessary in every area of life, but it can also be one of the hardest things for us to do. God is perfect, so any instruction from him is perfect. However, we may disagree with what He tells us to do or feel the need to question it. That was the case for me.

As you know, God told me not to pick up that man who assaulted my daughter. I kept questioning why God Himself would tell me not to pick up someone for church. As a Christian, it doesn't make sense. I reasoned myself out of obedience to God. Yes, I could've used the excuse that I was new to Christ, but there was a surety that the voice wasn't any other.

When it comes to the game of obedience, we may not be the ones who get the penalty. Being obedient to God doesn't need to make sense to us. God knows the end from the beginning; He sees everything, while we see only a little. I have forgiven the man who did what he did to my daughter, and I even had to check myself to ensure I indeed did. However, there wouldn't need to be a need for forgiveness if I had listened to God in the first place.

It took a lot for me to forgive. I was tormented for over 20 years with attacks on my mind. The scenario played over and over with me, constantly changing the outcome. It is too late to keep rehearsing what I should have done. I must move on and know that I forgive them and move forward. I opened up doors for myself and my daughter because of disobedience.

I can only thank God my youngest daughter grew up happy and healthy. She is a certified EMT/First Responder and loves helping people, especially the elderly. Don't let disobedience hurt you and the ones you love. Obey God, and it will be well with you and your house. Amen.

1 Samuel 15:22 "Behold, to obey is better than sacrifice, and to hearken than the fat of rams."

Prayer Point: Father God, thank you for speaking to me about my life. I pray that I will listen to you and obey your words every step of the way. I will not reason myself out of obedience based on what I think I know, and I will not make others sacrifice for my disobedience. I thank you, Father, in Jesus' name. Amen.

Proverbs 3:5-6 "Trust in the Lord with all your heart. Never rely on what you think you know. Remember the Lord in everything you do, and he will show you the right way."

Prayer Point: Father God, thank you for allowing me to trust you. I pray that I will do so and not rely on what I think I know. I will trust that if you tell me to do something, it is for my benefit and an example of your infinite wisdom. I thank you, Father, in Jesus' name. Amen.

John 16:13 "Howbeit when he, the Spirit of truth, is come, he will guide you into all truth: for he shall not speak of himself; but

whatsoever he shall hear, that shall he speak: and he will shew you things to come."

Prayer Point: Thank you, Father, for giving me the spirit of truth when I accepted your sacrifice on the cross. I know that the same spirit that guided Jesus is also in me. I pray that I will be obedient to the Holy Spirit and harken to its words always and forever, in Jesus' name. Amen.

Final Information: Additional Readings

As a final note, in a section I want to call the additional reading section, I want to refer to a book by Dr. Jerry and Carol Robeson titled "Strongman's His Name What's His Game?" In it, you will learn about multiple demonic influences, how they can enter someone's life, and how to deal with them.

What are strongholds exactly? Strongholds are similar to open doors. However, where strongholds are a way for something to get in, a castle is built that allows constant and continuous dwelling in someone's life. For example, if a thief enters your home and steals from you, that is an open door. If a thief decides to stay in your house, taking your money, happiness, and peace of mind, that is a stronghold.

Strongholds are not wholly evil; like bad open doors, there are good strongholds. A good stronghold has the opposite effect of a bad one; instead of a thief entering your home, imagine someone who is a counselor or a friend who decides to make their abode with you and helps you with every part of your life.

There are many scriptures in the Bible that show the importance of strongholds. However, I want us to focus on one particular scripture: 2 Corinthians 10:4.

2 Corinthians 10:4 "The weapons of the war we're fighting are not of this world but are powered by God and effective at tearing down the strongholds erected against His truth." (The Voice)

Here's some of the information from the book:

Spirit of Jealousy – (Murder, Revenge-Spite, Anger-Rage, Cruelty, Strife, Extreme Competition, Cause Divisions, Contention, Envy, Hatred, Jealousy – Numbers 5:14) (1 Corinthians 13; Ephesians 5:2; Galatians 5:19-21; Matthew 7:20);

Lying Spirit – (Strong Deception, Flattery, False Prophecy, Accusations, Religious Bondages, Superstitions, Gossip, False Teachers, Lies – 2 Chronicles 18:22) (John 14:17; 15:26; 16:13; Galatians 5:19-21; Matthew 7:20) Based on Matthew 18:18 Bind: Lying Spirit and Based on Matthew 18:19 Loose: Spirit of Truth (Jesus);

Perverse Spirit – (Broken Spirit, Evil Actions, Doctrinal Error, Twisting the Word, Chronic Worrier, Pornography, Rape, Incest, Contentious, Foolish, Sex Perversions, Child Abuse, Abortion, Atheist, Filthy Mind, Homosexual -Isaiah 19:14) (Zechariah 12:10; Hebrews 10:29; Galatians 5:19-21; Matthew 7:20) Based on Matthew 18:18 Bind: Perverse Spirit and Based on Matthew 18:19 Loose: God's Spirit; Pureness, Holiness;

We must first seek the Kingdom of God, where He will have us live because certain demons are assigned to different areas.

Spirit of Haughtiness – (Pride, Obstinate, Self-Righteous, Rebellion, Self-Deception, Idleness, Strife, Scornful, Arrogant-Smug, Rejection of the True and Living God-Jesus Christ – Proverbs 16:18) (Proverbs 16:19; Romans 1:4; Galatians 5:19-21; Matthew 7:20) based on Matthew 18:18 Bind: Spirit of Haughtiness (Pride) and based on Matthew 18:19 Loose: Humble & Contrite Spirit;

Spirit of Heaviness – (Excessive Mourning, Sorrow-Grief, Broken-Heart, Suicidal Thoughts, Self-Pity, Depression, Heaviness, Rejection, Insomnia, Despair-Dejection-Hopelessness, Inner Hurts-Torn Spirit – Isaiah 61:3) (John 15:26; Isaiah 61:3; Galatians 5:19-21; Matthew 7:20) and based on Matthew 18:18 Bind: Spirit of Heaviness and Based on Matthew 18:19 Loose: Comforter, Garment of Praise, Oil of Joy;

Spirit of Whoredoms – (Unfaithfulness/Adultery, Spirit, Soul or Body Prostitution, Love of Money - (Loving money more than you love the true and Living God -Jesus Christ), Fornication, Excessive Appetite, Worldliness, Chronic Dissatisfaction – Hosea 5:4) (Ephesians 3:16; Galatians 5:19-21; Matthew 7:20) and Based on Matthew 18:18 Bind: Spirit of Whoredoms and Based on Matthew 18:19 Loose: Spirit of God, Pure Spirit;

Spirit of Infirmity – (All kinds of sicknesses, diseases, hay-fever, allergies, asthma, arthritis, – is from the devil which is under the curse of the law (read Deuteronomy 28 & 30:19-20), Lingering Disorders, Weakness, Oppression, Impotent, Bent Body – Spine, Cancer – Frail – Lame – Luke 13:11-13) (Romans 8:2; 1 Corinthians 12:9; Galatians 5:19-21; Matthew 7:20) and Based on Matthew 18:18 Bind: Spirit of Infirmity and Based on Matthew 18:19 Loose: Spirit of Life & Gifts of Healing;

Spirit of Bondage – (Fears, Fear of Death, Compulsive Sin, Captivity to Satan, Servant of Corruption, Bondage to Sin, Selling Drugs (selling drugs, you are working for the devil to help him to steal, kill, and destroy the lives of the people), Additions (drugs, alcohol, cigarettes, food, etc. – Romans 8:15) (Galatians 5:19-21; Matthew 7:20) and based on Matthew 18:18 Bind: Spirit of Bondage and Based on Matthew 18:19 Loose: Liberty, Spirit of Adoption;

Spirit of Fear – (Fears-Phobias, Torment-Horror, Nightmares–Terrors, Fear of Man, Anxiety – Stress, Untrusting-Doubt, Fear of Death, Heart Attacks – 2 Timothy 1:7) (Galatians 5:19-21; Matthew 7:20) and based on Matthew 18:18 Bind: Spirit of Fear and based on Matthew 18:19 Loose: Love, Power & A Sound Mind;

Seducing Spirits – (Hypocritical Lies, Seared Conscience, Deception, Fascination to Evil Ways, Objects or Persons, Seducers-Enticers, Wander from Truth, Attractions – Fascination by False Prophets, signs and Wonders, etc. 1 Timothy 4:1) (John 16:13; Galatians 5:19-21; Matthew 7:20) and based on Matthew 18:18 Bind: Seducing Spirits and based on Matthew 18:19 Loose: Holy Spirit – Truth;

Spirit of Error – (Error, Unsubmissive, False Doctrines, Unteachable, Servant of Corruption, Contentions, Unteachable, Defensive/Argumentative (Defend "God's Revelations" to them personally – 1 John 4:6) (Psalm 51:10; Galatians 5:19-21; Matthew 7:20) and based on Matthew 18:18 Bind: Spirit of Error and based on Matthew 18:19 Loose: Spirit of Truth;

Spirit of Divination – (Fortuneteller-Soothsayer, Warlock-Witch, Sorcerer, Stargazer-Zodiac, Horoscopes, Hypnotist-Enchanter, Water Witching/Divination, Magic, Drugs, Rebellion) 1 Corinthians 12:9-12, Galatians 5:19-21, Matthew 7:20 – Acts 16:16-18) (1 Corinthians 12:9-

12; Galatians 5:19-21; Matthew 7:20) and based on Matthew 18:18 Bind: Spirit of Divination and Based on Matthew 18:19 Loose: Holy Spirit and Gifts;

Spirit of Anti-Christ – (Denies Deity of Christ, Denies Atonement, Anti-Christian, Lawlessness, Against Christ and His Teaching, Worldly Speech & Actions, Teacher of Heresies, Deceiver – 1 John 4:3) (1 John 4:6; Galatians 5:19-21; Matthew 7:20) and based on Matthew 18:18 Bind: Spirit of Anti-Christ and based on Matthew 18:19 Loose: Spirit of Truth;

Dumb and Deaf Spirit – (Dumb - Mute, Drown, Blindness, Suicidal, Burn, Mental Illness, Seizures/Epilepsy, Pining Away Prostration, Gnashing Teeth, Foaming at Mouth, Ear Problems, Tearing, Crying – Mark 9:17-29) (Romans 8:11; 1 Corinthians 12:9; Galatians 5:19-21; Matthew 7:20) and based on Matthew 18:18 Bind: Dumb and Deaf Spirit and based on Matthew 18:19 Loose: Resurrection Life & Gifts of Healing;

Familiar Spirit – (Necromancer, Peeping & Muttering, Clairvoyant, Drugs (GK. – Pharmakos), False Prophecy, Medium, Yoga, Spiritist, Passive Mind-Dreamers, False Prophecy – Leviticus 19:31) (1 Corinthians 12:9-12; Galatians 5:19-21; Matthew 7:20) and based on Matthew 18:18 Bind: Familiar Spirit and based on Matthew 18:19 Loose: Holy Spirit and Gifts.

As you can see, there are many things we need to be careful of. Although this may seem scary and intimidating, we can avoid all these things if we live by the Word.

Also, something that people heavily underestimate is the power of words. The Bible states that life and death are in the power of the tongue. We must start speaking and acting to open the right doors and close the wrong ones. Confession is not a one-time thing but a continual reaffirmation of something. So, continually reaffirm the word of God and refuse to speak evil. We are snared by the words that we speak. God created the universe with The Words that He had spoken and gave us the means to say the right ones – to close the wrong open doors forever.

About the Author

Tracey Lancaster was born and raised in the Washington, DC area. Living in the Southeast, she realized finishing school would have been impossible, so she moved in with her grandparents and completed High School. She has been working in the Federal Government for over 38 years. Being molested at an early age and looking for love in all the wrong places has caused her to make many bad choices and decisions until one day, she received Jesus Christ as her Lord and Savior. She attended Christian Bible College for 3-4 years at Jericho City of Praise. She started to grow up spiritually and mature in the Word of God. Being obedient to the voice of the Holy Spirit when she was instructed to write this book, she received her deliverance and healing from being molested and past abuse, hurt, rejection, and pain.

She is filled with the precious gift of the Holy Spirit. She is married to James Lancaster, and in their blended family, they have seven children (4 sons & 3 daughters), nine grandchildren (whom they call their Grand-buddies), and three daughters-in-law. Both she and her husband reside in Prince George's County. She is the President and founder of Jehovah-Jireh's Christian Clown and Balloon Ministry. She performs as a Christian clown at birthday parties, church functions, family reunions, and other events. She also has written many skits to exemplify the real issues she experienced in her past and to let God's people know they don't have to go down the wrong path or settle for anything less than God's best.

Her passion and heart desire is to be in God's perfect will and to be obedient to what He has called her to do. She is willing to go and do what He has called her to do regardless of how much of herself she has to expose to win souls for Jesus Christ.

Made in the USA
Middletown, DE
17 June 2024